get off
your knees &
pray

sheila walsh

THOMAS NELSON
Since 1798

NASHVILLE   DALLAS   MEXICO CITY   RIO DE JANEIRO

Published in Nashville, Tennessee, by Thomas Nelson. Thomas Nelson is a registered trademark of Thomas Nelson, Inc.

Thomas Nelson, Inc., titles may be purchased in bulk for educational, business, fund-raising, or sales promotional use. For information, please e-mail SpecialMarkets@ThomasNelson.com.

All Scripture quotations, unless otherwise indicated, are taken from The Holy Bible, New International Version®. © 1973, 1978, 1984, by International Bible Society. Used by permission of Zondervan Bible Publishing House. All rights reserved.

Scripture quotations noted NLT are taken from the *Holy Bible*, New Living Translation®, © 1996. Used by permission of Tyndale House Publishers, Inc., Wheaton, IL 60189. All rights reserved.

Scripture quotations noted NCV are taken from the *Holy Bible*, The New Century Version®. © 1987, 1988, 1991. Used by permission of Thomas Nelson Publishers.

Scripture quotations noted NKJV are taken from The New King James Version. All rights reserved. © 1982 by Thomas Nelson, Inc. Used by permission. All rights reserved.

Scripture quotations noted MSG are taken from *The Message* by Eugene H. Peterson. © 1993, 1994, 1995, 1996, 2000, 2001, 2002. Used by permission of NavPress Publishing Group. All rights reserved

ISBN. 978-1-4002-0253-9 (trade paper)

Library of Congress Cataloging-in-Publication Data

Walsh, Sheila, 1956–
    Get off your knees and pray / Sheila Walsh.
        p. cm.
    Summary: "A Woman's Guide to Life-Changing Prayer"—Provided by publisher.
    Includes bibliographical references.
    ISBN 978-0-8499-1953-4 (hardcover)
    ISBN 978-1-4002-8004-9 (IE)
    1. Prayer—Christianity. 2. Christian women—Religious life. I. Title.
BV210.3.W36 2007
248.3'2—dc22

                                                                    2007036803

Printed in the United States of America
10 11 12 13 14 RRD 9 8 7 6 5 4 3 2

This book is dedicated with love and gratitude
to our Women of Faith intercessor, Lana Bateman.
You have taught me so much about living a
life of prayer, and I thank our Father for you.

contents

Acknowledgments   vii

Introduction: God Is Listening   ix

part one: the path

1. What Does the Bible Actually Say about Prayer?   3
   Which of My Ideas Are from the Bible and Which Are
   from the "Church Lady"?

2. Why Is Prayer So Important?   16
   Does Prayer Really Help Me Grow?

3. Why Is It So Hard to Pray?   29
   If Prayer Really Matters So Much to God,
   Shouldn't It Be Easier to Do?

4. Do My Prayers Make a Difference?   43
   If God Has Already Decided What He Is Going to Do,
   Why Pray at All?

part two: the problem

5. Why Does God Say No?   59
   If God Is Loving and Kind, Why Doesn't He Give Me What I Want?

6. Is God Angry with Me?   69
   Will God Help Me if I'm the One Who Got Myself into This Mess?

7. Why Does God Seem Absent when I Pray?   81
   Why Does God Seem Near Sometimes and So Far Away at Others?

8. Why Did God Help Her but Not Me? 95
Does God Have Favorites?

part three: the plan

9. How Do I Know I Heard God's Voice? 113
Was It Him or Last Night's Pizza?

10. Can I Ask God for Anything if I Have Enough Faith? 125
Dear God, Will You Make Me Taller?

11. Can I Question God? 136
Is Anybody Out There?

12. Are You Asking Me to Let Go? 147
Falling Forward

part four: the purpose

13. Lay Your Burdens Down 161
The Gift of Confession

14. Pray It Forward 174
The Gift of Perseverance

15. Overwhelmed with Thanks 185
The Gift of Gratitude

16. And God Rejoiced 197
The Gift of Trust

17. You Are Not Alone 208
The Gift of Community

Conclusion: Prayer Is Who We Are 222
Notes 224

acknowledgments

All my most memorable trips have been shared with a friend or a loved one. Writing this book has been no exception.

I am deeply grateful to Leslie Peterson, who has walked this editorial path with me every step of the way. Your grace and patience touched me deeply, and your sense of humor carried me when I was about to shave my head!

Jennifer Stair took our offering and lovingly groomed and trimmed it so that even if it won't win Best in Show, it can wag its tail with the best of them.

Bryan Norman, you are my new hero. Your editorial suggestions, questions, wisdom, and encouragement have impacted me deeply. Thank you!

Brian Hampton and the whole Thomas Nelson team make it pure joy to follow the call of a writer. I consider it a great honor to be part of your family.

Tami Heim, you are a brilliant leader and treasured friend!

Mary Graham and my "porch pals" at Women of Faith—you are my fellow road warriors as we take the life-changing news of the love of God to a wounded world. I love you all.

I want to thank my husband, Barry, and son, Christian, for their grace, patience, and understanding of the writing process and for providing me with *so* much material!

God Is Listening

If you had asked me to describe my spiritual life when I was twenty years old, it would have sounded something like this: I love to read the Bible. I love reading spiritual classics. I am very involved in my church. And I am challenged in my prayer life.

At thirty, I would have said pretty much the same thing, except in regard to prayer I might have reduced "I am challenged" to "I stink." (I was beginning to be more honest about my life in my thirties.) But otherwise the facts would remain intact.

At forty, I would have added that I love talking to women about faith and fear, honesty and heartache. And I had pretty much resigned myself to "stinking" in my prayer life.

And now? Well, now I am fifty, and change in every arena of life has become an ongoing reality.

My eyesight has deteriorated to the shifting terrain of bifocals. At my last eye test, when the optometrist covered my left eye, I could only read the first two lines on the chart. When he covered my right eye, I couldn't see the wall!

I am definitely getting shorter. To remedy this, I have two clear choices: wear higher heels or have all my pants altered.

I need my roots retouched every three weeks now instead of every six. When I suggested going back to my natural color, my hair-stylist said I no longer have one. Who knew that was even possible?

But in the midst of all these unsettling changes, I am discovering profound and simple gifts that have come with the passing years. For example, I don't worry so much about the little things in life. If my son and four of his ten-year-old friends decide to make a fort in the kitchen just as I'm about to make dinner, I switch the menu to franks and beans and serve it to them in the tent. And when unexpected troubles come my way, I've learned I have good friends—friends I can count on. We love, treasure, and support one another. We laugh at all the petty indignities of aging and cry together when life takes one of us through a dark night.

I am changing in my understanding of my spiritual life too. I am more inclined to listen for God's voice than to present to him a list of requests. I have a quiet confidence that no matter what seems to be true, God is always in control.

Most important, I have realized that it is not possible to stink at prayer. It might feel that way to us at times, but I believe that from God's perspective, he gladly receives our words and he sees our hearts. Any prayer is a gift to him, for it means we are talking to him. We just have to take that first step—and begin embracing prayer as part of our daily lives, as vital to us as breathing.

I no longer divide my life into the spiritual part and everything else. I believe when we recognize God is always with us, every breath can be a prayer. Prayer is not just a few sentences we say to God while on our knees, but it is living out our ongoing, every-moment commitment to God—hence the title: *Get Off Your Knees and Pray!*

Perhaps you're thinking, *Prayer is easy—we were made to rejoice in our relationship with God and to thank him for his gifts.* Well, sure, it's always easy to be thankful for God's good gifts. But what about when we're not thankful? What about when we're hurt? Angry? Numb? Is it so easy then?

It might not be so easy, but he wants it to be our first response.

Or perhaps you're thinking, *Prayer has never been easy for me. I do stink at it!* You feel like what you say to him is insincere, unsure. Or you question whether he even really cares to hear from you. Or you're so overwhelmed you don't even want to talk to him.

It isn't. He does. He still wants you to.

God hears all our prayers, the good and the bad. He is big enough to handle our honest questions and our doubts and even our anger. I sat beside a friend after she buried her child and listened as she poured out her raw emotions to God. Her prayer wasn't pretty, but it was from her heart and God knew it. I watched my son struggle with prayer after the death of his beloved grandfather: "Didn't you tell me, Mommy, that if I prayed God would answer? Well, I asked him not to take my papa and he did. Prayer doesn't work!" It hurt me immeasurably to see his pain, but I knew God was there with him. And I've blasted God with my own prayer challenges . . . and mumbled to him my doubts. And I know he heard me. He has heard you too.

God receives our prayers—the thankful ones and the not-so-thankful ones, the eloquent ones and the less-than-perfect ones. He accepts not only our joyful prayers and self-confident prayers, but the prayers we offer when we're not certain of things—or when we're not sure we really want the answer. He accepts our anguished questioning when we experience trauma or loss. He even accepts the prayers that beg him to rain down disaster on someone who has wounded us (although he may not answer them). He accepts all our prayers because they acknowledge we believe he is in control. When we're happy, when we're angry, when we're hurting to the point that words are lost and all we can offer is a cry for help—he is still there.

God is listening.

This sharpening of my spiritual vision seemed to arrive at about the same time God deposited a seven-pound, eight-ounce beautiful baby boy into my arms. Becoming a mother ten years ago at forty affected my life in more ways than I imagined possible. (On a purely practical note, I now believe I should have slept more the first forty years!) As a new mom, I was humbled to realize that even the most insecure or guarded of us can love selflessly when we look into the eyes of our child. And I got a huge kick out of the fact that a girl like me, who was afraid of being beaten up on the school bus, could love my child so fiercely that I would rip the legs off a lion if it came near my son.

But more than that, having a child changed the way I viewed my relationship—my ongoing prayer conversation—with God.

I remember my friend Amy Grant saying that when her first son, Matt, was born, she realized that for the rest of her life her heart would walk outside of her body. I didn't understand the accuracy of that statement until my son, Christian, was born. Since then my life has changed in obvious ways and in ways that are more difficult to articulate.

Often, when Christian is asleep at night, I will stand at the side of his bed and marvel at the gift he is to me. I began this practice when he was just a baby. Before motherhood I had no idea that I could feel the depth of love that would consider any kind of sacrifice a privilege. But as I watched over my son, I came to an acute new awareness of our heavenly Father watching over us. And I began to understand the depth of his love for us.

Because of this, my prayer life changed. I loved talking to and listening to God. I loved talking to him all the time. (I still do!) And being honest with him. Being a sleep-deprived mother of a baby in those early days eliminated much of the preamble in my conversation with God; I just got right to the point.

Having my son face a life-threatening illness sharpened my dialogue too. Further tests revealed he was anemic rather than suffering from leukemia, but being in that terrifying place for a few days changed me. I was not so careful about the potential of offending God. I was afraid, I was angry, and I was honest. It felt good to relate to God in that authentic way.

It still does. I could never go back to my old, edited prayers. I think it would be a huge insult to God. Raw emotion declares that you trust him with everything that is in you, knowing he will still be there when the outburst is over. When I share my fear and my anger and my uncertainty when it is most acute, I also pour out my love and gratitude with more passion. Real relationship demands intimate dialogue. Even if it's just lying facedown on the carpet calling out his name with your last ounce of strength.

Within the pages of this book is an invitation to pour yourself out—heart and soul—to God, to experience what I've come to know and embrace. I spent so much of my life trying to be "good enough" for God. I wanted to get all my spiritual ducks in a row before I came to him. That is a lonely way to live. We have been created for intimate conversation with our Father. The greatest source of joy and peace in my life today is the absolute conviction that I can come to God as I am and be loved and accepted. I can tell God my hopes and dreams, share my disappointments and hurts.

This invitation comes with a disclaimer, however: I don't profess to have all knowledge. Much about prayer is still a mystery to me. I have more questions than I have answers: Can we change God's mind? . . . If God is sovereign and has already set everything in place, why bother praying? . . . Why does it seem as if some people's prayers are answered and others' are not? . . . How does the level of my faith affect the outcome of my prayers?

Yes, there are many questions, but that's okay. My plea to you even in the midst of the questions is simple: talk to God and take time to listen. No matter how "vertically challenged" we may believe ourselves to be, God is listening and talking to us all the time. We only need to learn to stop and listen.

We are living in difficult times. War and terrorism are no longer a million miles away from home. Cancer and heart disease are waging an unprecedented battle against younger and younger people. The financial "golden days" of the 1980s are long gone. People worry if they will have enough savings to help their children through college or if they themselves will have enough to retire on. The bottom line is, life is hard.

God knows all about it. And more than that, right in the center of the tornado of our lives, he offers a quiet place, a shelter where he waits with open arms and an open heart to embrace any of us who will come. Whether you are young or old, full of hope or full of fear, angry or excited, bitter or grateful, this remains my conviction: God is listening.

So let's begin this journey and explore how to recognize the hand of God in every moment. Whether we're on or off our knees—let's pray!

part 1

the
path

What Does the Bible Actually Say about Prayer?

Which of My Ideas Are from the Bible and Which Are from the "Church Lady"?

To be a Christian without prayer is no more possible than to be alive without breathing. —Martin Luther

Be joyful always; pray continually; give thanks in all circumstances, for this is God's will for you in Christ Jesus. —1 Thessalonians 5:16–18

My ten-year-old son, Christian, is very computer literate, as are most fifth graders these days. Last Thanksgiving he saw me staring at a large, frozen turkey on the kitchen counter. Immediately assessing I had cooking issues, he said, "Just Google it, Mom."

"I beg your pardon?" I replied, eyeing the forbidding frosty fowl.

"If you're not sure what to do, just Google it," he said. "That always works for me."

So Google it I did, and I found the cooking instructions I needed.

Now, I realize I may have lost you already. If you are not

computer savvy, I empathize. I still find it hard to believe I can pick up a piece of plastic—commonly called a telephone—punch in a few numbers, and in seconds be talking to my mother on the west coast of Scotland. But it doesn't stop there. Life marches on at an unbridled pace these days. Now I can go online with my laptop, use a search engine like Google, punch in "Help me! My turkey is still frozen!" and within moments receive the message, "You should have taken it out last night, you moron!" (No, not actually. What I did receive was a very detailed plan for thawing and cooking an award-winning roast beast.)

Google and other online search engines have not only brought the world to our doorstep, but they have also taken us to the world. Before I left for Nairobi, Kenya, in December 2006, I set up Google Earth on my laptop for Christian. Each evening he could log on and, with the punch of a few keys, locate a live shot of our house in Frisco, Texas. Then he could type in my location in Africa, and the satellite would pull out as the globe on the screen spun to Africa and focused on where I was that day.

Wow! The world is getting smaller every day. In many ways that's a good thing, but in other ways not so much. Take prayer, for example. Since nowadays just about anyone can reach out and touch us, we're being bombarded from all directions with a hodgepodge of ideas on how to relate to God.

Out of curiosity, I decided to Google the word *prayer*. I couldn't believe the response—a smorgasbord offered in the name of communion with almighty God. One website detailed a free mini course that would teach me about the "seven spirits of God." Another site offered telephone miracles twenty-four hours a day that would enhance my health, my finances, and my relationships.

One interesting site even showed me pictures of what prayer should look like. It said if I was a Christian, I should bow my head and clasp my hands together. If I was a Native American, I should dance; if a Hindu, chant; if a Sufi, whirl. If I was an Orthodox Jew, I should sway, and if I was a Quaker . . . I should be quiet!

THE WISDOM OF THE YOUNG

Googling *prayer* proved to be more confusing than helpful, so I asked some of my son's friends this simple question: "What does the Bible say about prayer?" Their responses were interesting, to say the least. Here are a few:

- "Don't even try it if you're mad with your dad—God won't be listening."

- "Wash your hands first!"

- "Remember to say amen or everyone's food will get cold!"

- "Think about others before you think about yourself."

- "Just concentrate on God and try not to fall asleep."

Hmm. Not quite what I'd been looking for. Their answers conveyed that there are right things to do and wrong things to do when we pray—and you'd better get it right if you even have a hope of God listening to you! Their responses also seemed to indicate that they had been corrected in their past efforts at prayer and were working with a fresh set of ground rules.

But something besides their responses jumped out at me. Interestingly, the boys' tone of voice changed when I asked them about prayer. Even my own animated son became a Francis of Assisi as he responded—quiet, gentle, reverent. (I have to tell you, however, that moment soon passed.) This indicated to me that even at a young age, we're conditioned to believe that fellowship with God is some sort of lofty and theological transaction. The boys' attitude mirrored what they had seen others do in an attempt to be "religious." They had no clue how to answer the question accurately, but they sure did put on a good show while they were talking about it!

When I thought about it, I had to confess I've sometimes done the same. And I'm sure you have too. Think about it—how many times have we been asked to pray in public and, instead of talking with God using the manner and words we offer at home, we find our "spiritual" voices, religious vocabulary, and pious pose?

Surely that can't be how God wants us to relate to him. So what does the Bible actually tell us about prayer? It seemed a good time to go to the source and investigate.

WHAT DOES THE BIBLE TELL US ABOUT PRAYER?

As I pored over the Scriptures, searching for what God has to say about prayer, several things became immediately clear:

⋅> We are called to pray with a *clean heart*: "If I regard iniquity in my heart, the Lord will not hear. But certainly

God has heard me; He has attended to the voice of my prayer" (Psalm 66:18–19 NKJV).

•> We are called to pray, *believing*: "And whatever things you ask in prayer, believing, you will receive" (Matthew 21:22 NKJV).

•> We are called to pray *in Christ's name*: "And whatever you ask in My name, that I will do, that the Father may be glorified in the Son" (John 14:13 NKJV).

•> We are called to pray according to *the Father's will*: "Now this is the confidence that we have in Him, that if we ask anything according to His will, He hears us" (1 John 5:14 NKJV).

On second thought, even with these "clear" instructions, I still had questions. So I took a closer look at these four directives.

A Clean Heart

According to Psalm 66:18, our purity of heart is so essential that if we "regard iniquity in [our] heart, the Lord will not hear" (NKJV). And in Psalm 51:10, David urges God to give him "a clean heart" (NKJV).

What exactly is a "clean heart"? How clean, exactly? Scrubbed-spotless-till-you-can-see-your-reflection clean? Or quick-tidy-up-before-the-guests-arrive clean?

As women, our hormones lead us on a lively dance for most of our lives. So what do we do on those "days of the month" when we don't feel very holy or sometimes even sane? Does God hear our prayers when our emotions are taking us on a roller coaster ride? What if we want to have a clean heart, but we're having trouble with it? What if we *believe* we have a clean heart, but there is some little seed of unforgiveness buried deep inside us we've forgotten all about? Are we only responsible for the sins we remember or for every little offense we've committed over our entire lifetime?

I received a letter from a woman who had been sexually abused by her father when she was a child. Her concern was that there were months of this devastating time in her childhood she had blocked out. She simply couldn't remember what had happened. "How can I come to God with a clean heart when I can't remember so much of that horrible time? Will God hold that against me?" she asked.

My heart ached for this woman who had already suffered so much and was now tormented by the thought that the offenses acted out upon her would hinder her prayers and follow her for the rest of her life. I wanted to tell her that part of the miracle of prayer is that God knows what we need before we even ask him. When it is our earnest desire to be clean, he sees that—whether we can remember every detail of our lives or not. Yes, he wants us to come before him with a pure heart, but he also tells us that he hears our honest petitions. Notice what verse 19 of Psalm 66 says: "Certainly God has heard me."

We can't keep worrying about how clean the corners of our soul are. If we get caught up in that whirlpool of self-loathing and doubt, we're only headed down. But if we come before the God who makes all things new, believing in faith that he knows our true hearts, we are certain to be uplifted.

Believing

Surely Jesus' words recorded in Matthew 21:22 have caused much confusion among believers: "And whatever things you ask in prayer, believing, you will receive." "Whatever" covers a lot of ground.

Perhaps you have been exposed to prosperity teaching, which seems to advocate "if you can name it, you can claim it; if you can mark it, you can park it!" This theology is not an accurate understanding of what the Bible teaches. Prosperity teaching takes the wonderful truth that our Father is the King of kings and reduces it to the conclusion that we should all then live like royalty on this earth.

For instance, I was channel surfing one night and landed on a religious talk show. Three college students were being interviewed about their faith. One girl held up a picture of a red Mercedes convertible and announced proudly that this was what she was "believing" for. As though that's what Jesus had in mind for her!

But beyond the self-indulgent misinterpretations of this verse is a much more serious heart cry from those who long for God to intervene when life is falling apart and who can't understand why he doesn't appear to hear their prayers. From 1987 to 1992, I was cohost of *The 700 Club* with Dr. Pat Robertson. I received hundreds of letters from viewers who stumbled over this misunderstanding of prayer. They said things like:

> "I prayed in faith that my husband would be healed of cancer, but he died. What did I do wrong?"

> "I have given and given to the church and this ministry believing for a miracle in my own finances, but I am still in debt. What am I doing wrong?"

⋅❯ "I have kept myself pure and prayed, believing that God would bring me a husband, and I am still alone. Why isn't God honoring my prayers?"

I witnessed such torment in people's lives. Many felt they were doing something wrong, and if they could just find out what the key was, things would been different. Can you imagine the agony of believing your child or your husband would not have died if you had somehow worked out this puzzle in time? Or the pain of the woman who sits home alone wondering where her soul mate is as she watches the years pass by, taking with them her ability to be a mother?

To these situations, add the agony of silence. If you believe that somehow whatever reality you are living in is your fault, who do you dare talk to? How can you voice these things aloud and risk seeing disapproval in the eyes of someone else?

I think this verse has left many sitting alone and lost. I'll be honest: there's no easy answer. But I think that part of the problem is we tend to focus on only one part of that scripture. We want to hear all about the "receiving" side of things—*What are you going to do for me, God? Why haven't you given me what I asked for?*—rather than the "believing" side—*God, I believe in you 100 percent and know you love me, and today that's all that matters.* God has and always will have our best interests at heart. Just as our children look at us in faith, knowing we love them and will take care of them, we need to do the same with our heavenly Father. I'm not saying that will always be easy; we might want to stomp our foot or cry into our pillows. But we have to trust that God will make all things clear some day.

In Jesus' Name

In John's gospel we read that whatever prayers we ask *in Jesus' name* will be answered so that God the Father will be glorified (14:13). This is such an incredible gift. But . . . the authority we're given can be a dangerous thing. I think it's easy to tag, "In Jesus' name, amen" to the end of our prayers without thinking through the full implications of what that means.

Coming in someone's name means you represent that person —you have been granted the authority to speak for them. For example, when police officers or FBI agents present themselves at someone's home, they produce identification to show that they have the authority of the agency they represent behind them. Likewise, when we say, "In Jesus' name," we are saying we are on royal business. Understanding that has helped me be bold in prayer but also be careful that my requests are in keeping with the character of Christ. I have a fresh sense of what an honor it is to be able to come to God in his Son's name, and I work hard to not abuse the privilege.

According to the Father's Will

In John's first letter, he clarifies that we are to ask according to the *Father's will,* and he will hear us (5:14). What exactly does that mean? How do we keep from replacing his wishes with our own? Even more, how do we even know what the Father's will is in any given situation? To my human understanding, it would always seem to be God's will to heal a child or a broken marriage. Wouldn't such a miracle bring glory to God? What about when a child prays a simple prayer of faith in Jesus' name? Surely God would answer that.

My son faced this heartbreaking dilemma when he was just four years old. My father-in-law, William Pfaehler, lived with us for two years after the death of his wife, Eleanor. Having him in our home was a wonderful gift to all of us, but especially to Christian. He loved his papa so much, and they had a lot of fun together. One night when my husband, Barry, was in Florida, William had a heart attack and collapsed in his bathroom. Christian and I sat with him until the paramedics arrived. He was still breathing when they loaded him into the ambulance, but his lips were very blue. Christian and I followed the ambulance to the hospital. When we arrived, the doctor informed us that William had not survived the trip.

Christian was quiet as we drove home. All he said that night was, "I'm going to miss my papa."

He grieved openly for weeks, and then one day I saw a flash of anger cross his face as he brushed our cat, Lily, off the sofa. I suggested that we take a walk, and I asked him if he was angry. With his customary honesty, he told me he was.

"You told me, Mom, that Jesus listens to our prayers and answers them. Well, I asked God not to take my papa, and he did anyway. So what's the point?"

I felt my son's pain. (Is there a believer alive who hasn't thought that when it seemed as if heaven was silent to his or her cries?) At his tender age, my son had to experience what it means to pray according to the Father's will, whether or not he—or I—understood it.

There is obviously much more to this thing called *prayer* than what we currently know. Though you and I will be gathering information about prayer all our days, our lives are only a speck of time in God's plan. There's no way we could hope to understand everything in our limited time on earth.

Of course, that doesn't stop us from trying to figure it out, does it? Sometimes we're tempted to think we know all the answers—or at least most of them. We draw conclusions from our limited perceptions and try to force ourselves and others into believing them.

THE CHURCH LADY

If you were a fan of the television show *Saturday Night Live* in the late eighties, you might remember a character created by Dana Carvey. Her name was Enid Strict, affectionately referred to as the Church Lady. She was the very prim, proper, and pious host of a talk show called *Church Chat.* As she interviewed celebrities, the Church Lady used her platform to rail against their ungodly behavior.

Carvey says he based the character on women from the church he attended while he was growing up who would keep track of his and others' attendance.[1] I find that very sad. I wonder how many people have encountered a Church Lady growing up, and because of her strict views, they think God judges them according to their church attendance. That he answers their prayers based upon their adherence to rules defined by culture more than by Scripture. I can't imagine many people would want to pour out their heart to someone like that. In the hands of someone like Enid Strict, prayer is a weapon to be used against people: "Sic 'em, God!"

Prayer is not always easy. Nor is it always joyful. And no, we don't always get what we hope for out of the dialogue. What I do firmly reject, however, is the idea that God is a cruel puzzle maker who watches dispassionately to see if we will figure things out in time. That goes against the whole story revealed through the Word of God.

From the first words of Genesis until the glorious conclusion at the end of the Revelation to John, what flows from every page of Scripture is one grand prayer adventure. It is a love story about a God who chooses relationship rather than blind obedience, who allowed his only Son to be tortured and killed so that you and I could be washed clean of the sin that separates us from him. God does not torture his beloved people. He calls to them.

Perhaps in this first chapter I have found more questions than answers, but I am convinced of one thing—it matters that we pray. After all, Jesus didn't say *if* you pray but *when* you pray (Matthew 6:5).

What a Friend we have in Jesus,
all our sins and griefs to bear!
What a privilege to carry
everything to God in prayer!
O what peace we often forfeit,
O what needless pain we bear,
All because we do not carry
everything to God in prayer.

Have we trials and temptations?
Is there trouble anywhere?
We should never be discouraged;
take it to the Lord in prayer.

Can we find a friend so faithful
who will all our sorrows share?
Jesus knows our every weakness;
take it to the Lord in prayer.

Are we weak and heavy laden,
cumbered with a load of care?
Precious Savior, still our refuge,
take it to the Lord in prayer.
Do your friends despise, forsake you?
Take it to the Lord in prayer!
In His arms He'll take and shield you;
you will find a solace there.

Blessed Savior, Thou hast promised
Thou wilt all our burdens bear
May we ever, Lord, be bringing all to
Thee in earnest prayer.
Soon in glory bright unclouded there
will be no need for prayer
Rapture, praise and endless worship will be
our sweet portion there.
—JOSEPH M. SCRIVEN

Why Is Prayer So Important?

Does Prayer Really Help Me Grow?

Prayer does not change God, but it changes him who prays. —Søren Kierkegaard

Surely I spoke of things I did not understand, things too wonderful for me to know. "You said, 'Listen now, and I will speak, I will question you, and you shall answer me.' My ears had heard of you but now my eyes have seen you. Therefore I despise myself and repent in dust and ashes." —Job 42:3–6

Both of my grandfathers died before I was born. But my mom tells a story about her father that I think is hilarious.

From what I understand, my grandfather was a hardworking man with a simple faith. At mealtimes, his standard grace was: "For what we are about to receive, may the Lord make us truly thankful." But on one particular occasion when they were having guests for lunch after church, my nana asked him to embellish the usual blessing a bit.

He must have forgotten her request, because he started out as he always did: "For what we are about to receive, may the Lord make us truly thankful."

There was a noticeable pause before he added, "And make me a good boy, amen!"

Now, at this point my granddad must have been in his sixties—but I guess that's the only other prayer he could remember from his childhood. I am so sorry I wasn't there. I would have fallen off my chair in hysterics, high-fiving my granddad on the way down!

My nana wanted my granddad to come up with a few more impressive words, but I am convinced that the words we use are of less interest to God than the intent of our hearts. God hears our heart no matter the words we use.

But my grandfather's simple—if unexpected!—prayer begs a question: does the actual act of prayer, of throwing ourselves on the mercy and grace of God, change us? Was there a kernel of truth in my granddad's faltering prayer—that just by being in God's presence, we become "better" boys and girls?

I think one of the most powerful books in the Bible to support and perhaps answer that question is Job. I base that assertion on the verse I quoted at the beginning of this chapter: "My ears had heard of you but now my eyes have seen you" (42:5). This is a very short sentence in a very long book, but for me it contains the whole point of Job's story. Job says (and this is my paraphrase): "God, I knew about you before, I knew of all the marvelous things you have done. But now that I have been in the ring with you for several rounds, I have a completely different kind of relationship with you and a new understanding of your greatness."

That's one of the many things I find interesting about Job's story—he is described in such glowing terms at the beginning of the story and yet admits he has room to learn. This is not a story of a treacherous man who encountered God and was converted by the experience. It's the story of a godly man who through tragedy and very bitter dialogue with God came to a whole new understanding of who God is. In other words, he wasn't a man who was changed from "bad" to "good." He was a man changed from "good" to "better"!

I long for that for each one of us. More specifically, I thirst for that in my own life—that my prayer life would become so vibrant, intense, and moment-by-moment I cannot help but be changed.

Let's look at what happened to Job that thrust him from a man who honored God while remaining in control of his own life to a man on his face clinging to God with nothing left but truth.

LIFE CHANGES IN A MOMENT

The story of Job begins like this: "There was a man in the land of Uz, whose name was Job; and that man was blameless and upright, and one who feared God and shunned evil" (Job 1:1 NKJV).

Many scholars and theologians study the book of Job within the context of human suffering, and for very good reason. His story contains every element of heartache that could decimate a soul.

Job was a morally upright man. He had seven sons, three daughters, and a large acreage of land for his livestock. Indeed, he was one of the wealthiest men in the world at that time. "His possessions were seven thousand sheep, three thousand camels, five hundred yoke of oxen, five hundred female donkeys, and a very large household, so that this man was the greatest of all the people of the East" (1:3 NKJV).

Yet in the course of one day, Job lost everything. His children were killed by a freak accident, and his livestock carried away by enemies. All his servants were slaughtered, apart from one left with the horrible job of conveying the news to his boss.

Job's response was amazing. Like any of us might do, he ripped his robe, shaved his head, and fell to the ground as grief washed over him in waves. But this is what he said: "The LORD gave, and the LORD has taken away; blessed be the name of the LORD" (1:21 NKJV). I'm sure he prayed that sacrificial prayer with tears pouring down his face, but he prayed it anyway.

Job's wife wasn't able to understand how her husband could still honor God in the face of such tragedy. She suggested that he curse God and die.

Now, this woman has been maligned in many sermons and books, but I have to say I have great empathy for Job's wife. I pray that if tragedy were to strike my family, by God's grace I would share Job's heart. But I'm not sure I would get there in day one. Job's wife had borne their ten children. She'd carried each one for nine months, given birth, fed them, and held them when they cried at night. Within one moment, they were all gone. In her day, children and wealth were seen as signs of God's favor. I can't blame her for assuming God was done with them.

Job, however, was not convinced. We read that in all that happened that day Job did not sin or charge God with any wrong (1:22). He recognized the great evil and disaster, but he didn't blame God. Job knew God does not rain down disaster on his children.

But don't think that held Job back from sharing his raw emotions with God. As the book progresses, Job puts everything he ever held to be true on the table of his soul and reexamines it, at times bitterly. Job obviously felt able to pour out the agony that weighed him down.

Which was a good thing, since each of his hopefully well-meaning friends added to his pain, intensifying his anger with easy answers. Why is it that we so often forget our tongues when comforting others? As my friend Barbara Johnson often says, "When pain is at its freshest, words should be fewest."

I remember spending time with a mom who had lost her child on that brutal day in 1999 when twelve students and a teacher at Columbine High School in Littleton, Colorado, were shot and killed. She told me that at the memorial service for her child, someone asked her what she was going to do with her daughter's bedroom now.

Thoughtless words are like salt rubbed into an open wound. Job gave us insights into what he thought about the ones spoken to him by his wife and friends.

What is interesting for us as readers of Job's story is that we are shown a side of the story he never knew. It's as if we are watching as a play unfolds, and we see and hear things the main character is unaware of. On a side stage, Satan told God Job was only loyal to him because life was so good. He claimed that if God took away all the things Job loved and counted on, then Job would curse God to his face.

I have always struggled with God's response. Instead of dismissing Satan from his presence, God allowed him to attack Job's family and his wealth. There have been many wonderful books written on the book of Job, so I will not attempt to summarize their content here. But let me just say that if Satan came to me and asked to mess with my family, I fear my response would not follow God's pattern as nicely as Job's did.

I say this because I know—I've been through my own times of testing.

I CAN'T DO THIS, LORD!

Pain has a way of reducing conversations with God to what matters and what we know to be true. I can think of several situations in my own life where being intentionally engaged in prayer was life changing. I have written about several of them before, so I won't spend much time on them here.[1] But if we are new friends, I want you to understand what a profound impact one of these painful times had on my prayer life and relationship with my Father.

I was thirty-eight years old when Barry and I married, so we were aware we might not be able to have children. We were therefore very elated when in 1996, at age forty, I became pregnant with my first and only (so far) child.

Of course, almost immediately doubt started creeping in—at least for me. I knew Barry would be a great dad. He loves kids, and I'd watched how children eagerly responded to him.

But never having done this parenting thing before, I wasn't so sure about myself. I knew I would be a good mother, because I would *choose* to be. (And I'm nothing if not determined when I've set my mind to something!) I just didn't know if I would feel all the things other mothers appear to feel. I've never been one to want to hold other people's children. At the time I didn't realize that on the day my son was born, a part of me would be born as well.

I enjoyed my pregnancy even though I threw up from morning until night for the first trimester. Time passed quickly, and one day the ultrasound showed we were going to have a boy. It was great news to both of us. I remember leaving the doctor's office that day and driving to a store in Laguna Beach, California, where we were living at the time, and buying six blue outfits.

Life was perfect.

Until, in a moment, our path took a sudden, sharp left turn. My doctor called and said she thought something was wrong with the baby. She wanted to do an amniocentesis. I didn't want to have this procedure done, but she talked me into it, saying that when it came time to deliver the baby, she would know what she was dealing with.

It was a very different experience to lie on the same table we'd had the ultrasound on and bring up the image of our baby again—this time not to determine sex but to make sure the needle withdrawing the amniotic fluid didn't touch him. I cried all the way home and then we waited for news. I'm not good at waiting, but I had no choice.

When my doctor called, it was with bad news: there was definitely something wrong with the baby, but we wouldn't know the extent until he was born.

I cried and Barry cried. We decided not to tell our families for a while. They had just received the great news that it was a boy, and we didn't want to take that joy away. Barry is an only child, so our son would be his parents' first grandchild.

For the next few weeks we just carried on as normal. But I began to feel a subtle shift in my heart toward God. I was getting angry. I held it in for a while until one day, early in the morning, when I went for a walk along the beach. I was on a quiet, lonely stretch, so I was able to vent my feelings.

Why did you do this, God?

Why did you let me get pregnant if you knew this would happen?

Is this just one more thing that you are asking me to experience so I can better understand other women when they suffer? If it is, I quit!

If I had your power, I would never let those I love suffer!

I can't do this, Lord!

I realize these prayers might be disturbing to some who have never believed it appropriate to question God. But I'm not relating my story for sensationalism; it's not my heart to shock people, but just to tell the truth. At that time in my life, that's where I found myself: at a moment of mistrust in God. I felt so out of control, and that really scared me.

Be truthful—haven't you ever felt the same way? Have you ever been desperate to regain control when your life has taken a drastic and unexpected turn? I imagine so. After all, our world is imperfect.

But God understands and allows our doubt. Why? Because if we use it productively in our relationship with God, it changes us.

Yes, there is something to Satan's allegation that when Job's life was going smoothly, it was relatively easy for him to maintain a grateful attitude to God. What Satan didn't realize, though, is that when we humans dig deep into our soul and pour out our heart, even in bitterness, God is there and we come to know him more deeply than ever before.

I remember thinking, *Well, this is where the rubber meets the road. Either this God I have been following since I was eleven years old is big*

*enough to handle my questions, fear, and anger—or he is not almighty
God. I need to know.*

So I tested him. I questioned his will. And every time I expressed
to him my fear and weakness, he was there with me. At first I
didn't want to acknowledge his presence, as if by doing so I was saying I accepted what was going on. In some strange way it was almost
as if I thought my protests would keep the pain away.

But even though I continued to struggle, I was deeply aware of
God's comfort and understanding. And in time, I opened my
heart to what he was speaking to me. All the scriptures that had
been tucked into my heart since I was a child now became like my
literal daily sustenance:

⇢ "The LORD is on my side; I will not fear" (Psalm 118:6
NKJV).

⇢ "The LORD is my light and my salvation; whom shall I
fear? The LORD is the strength of my life; of whom shall
I be afraid?" (Psalm 27:1 NKJV).

⇢ "Don't be afraid, I've redeemed you. I've called your
name. You're mine. When you're in over your head, I'll
be there with you. When you're in rough waters, you
will not go down. When you're between a rock and a
hard place, it won't be a dead end—because I am God,
your personal God, The Holy of Israel, your Savior. I
paid a huge price for you: . . . That's how much you
mean to me! That's how much I love you! I'd sell off the
whole world to get you back, trade the creation just for
you" (Isaiah 43:1–4 MSG).

And slowly but surely, as the weeks passed, I found a strength I hadn't had before. It was nothing to do with me. I didn't see myself as any stronger than I was before. In fact, quite the opposite. I became aware that God was right beside me and that when I fell down, he would pick me up. He imparted his own strength to me.

I DIDN'T UNDERSTAND

When Christian was born on Friday, December 13, 1996, at 5:20 a.m., he came into the world as a perfect baby boy. Two weeks prior to his birth, my doctor called and told me that the results of my amniocentesis test had come back with the results of another forty-year-old patient, and our files had been misplaced—my results went into her file and hers to mine.

My initial response was elation; I was so happy to know that Christian was going to be okay. But even as I picked up the phone to tell Barry the great news, I stopped for a moment. I suddenly realized that somewhere there was another mother receiving a very different call. I fell to my knees and prayed for her. I wondered who she was and if she knew the Savior. I knew that the doctor would not be able to tell me her name, but I wept for her. I wondered, too, if God in his sovereignty had allowed me to carry her burden for the previous months. I will never know.

You could choose to say that all my fear, all my doubt, all my questioning of God was therefore in vain. But you'd be wrong. I know that this intense time changed me. Three years later, we faced another scare with Christian. Although this also proved to be a false alarm, for the short time Christian was undergoing tests for leukemia and we were waiting for the results, I had a keen awareness of God's presence. I was still afraid, but my heart was thrown open to God knowing that whatever we faced, he would carry us through. I had learned how to talk to God and listen for his voice all day. I had always needed him that much, but I hadn't been aware of that need.

Just the same, Job is a different man at the end of his story than the man we met at the beginning. The man we first met was a good, honorable man. He was obviously a good business man, a leader, and a good father.

But as we walk with him through the devastating losses and the loss of his own physical health, we see Job question why he was even born. We see how he cries out to God for answers. And then, gloriously, we see how God answers him. For just a moment, it is as if God pulls back the curtain that divides heaven and earth and allows Job to catch a glimpse of his greatness. Job is completely overwhelmed by this revelation. As the visible world is kissed by the invisible, Job is given access to the bigger picture and is forever changed by it.

What is unseen is far more real than what we can see with human eyes, and Job was given the gift of a glimpse into our eternal reality. I believe that one of the most profound differences prayer makes in us is just that—understanding the bigger picture. Job's losses threw him onto his knees and then his face. When he was finally able to stand again, he was a different person. And so was I. It is not possible to experience that kind of a dramatic revelation of the character and power of God and remain the same.

Prayer is our lifeline between the physical world we can see and the spiritual world that is our eternal reality. Prayer transforms us by making us "better" boys and girls, as my grandfather alluded to, and by "better" I mean we remember what is true as opposed to what may appear to be true in the moment. I think of "better" in the context of having our vision focused and our hearing fine-tuned as we come face to face with a God who can move not only mountains but our own hearts. But if prayer is so key to our lives as believers, if it is so powerful a tool in God's hands to change us—why is it so hard to do?

Through the love of God our Savior,
All will be well;
Free and changeless is His favor;
All, all is well.
Precious is the blood that healed us;
Perfect is the grace that sealed us;
Strong the hand stretched out to shield us;
All must be well.

Though we pass through tribulation,
All will be well;
Ours is such a full salvation;
All, all is well.
Happy still in God confiding,
Fruitful, if in Christ abiding,
Holy through the Spirit's guiding,
All must be well.

We expect a bright tomorrow;
All will be well;

Faith can sing through days of sorrow,
All, all is well.
On our Father's love relying,
Jesus every need supplying,
Or in living, or in dying,
All must be well.
—MARY B. PETERS

Why Is It So Hard to Pray?

*If Prayer Really Matters So Much to God,
Shouldn't It Be Easier to Do?*

When a doctoral student at Princeton asked, "What is there left in the world for original dissertation research?" Albert Einstein replied, "Find out about prayer. Somebody must find out about prayer." —QUOTED IN *LEADERSHIP JOURNAL* (WINTER 1983)

Cast your burden on the LORD, and He shall sustain you; He shall never permit the righteous to be moved. —PSALM 55:22 NKJV

January 13, 2007, is a day I will never forget. It's the day my son, Christian, ran away from home. Now, I have always known that was a possibility. When my brother, Stephen, was about Christian's age, he would threaten to take off every now and again. He would pack his little suitcase with all his most treasured items and sit it at the door—as a warning, I'm sure. He never actually left, but the threat was there.

What I hadn't anticipated with Christian was that he would let me know he was going.

It was just after lunch, and I was clearing the table when he asked me if he could have a flask of hot chocolate. I asked him if he was heading out to play soccer, and he replied, "No, Mom. I'm running away from home."

"Wow! That's huge," I said. "Do you have any idea where you might go?"

"North, I think. . . . Yes, I'll head north," he replied.

"North is good," I said. "I've always liked north. Do you mind me asking why you're going now? You know, at this point in your life?"

"Think about it, Mom. Nothing ever happens here. There's you and Dad and the two dogs. That's it! How will I ever have stories to tell?" he said.

"Good point," I agreed. "What will you do for money?"

"I think I'll come home on weekends," he replied.

"Well, that's great," I said. "What else do you need?"

"I'll take a couple of good books, the dogs' blanket, some Cheetos . . . and I think I'll take the soft pellet gun Dad got me for Christmas."

"That would be a big 'No' on the gun," I said. "You are only allowed to use that with adult supervision."

He looked very disheartened. "What will I do if there are snakes?" he asked.

"Pour hot chocolate on them," I suggested. "I hear they hate that."

Finally Christian's backpack was full, and he gave me a big hug before he headed out the back door.

"Where will your first stop be?" I asked.

"I think I'll stop by the big old tree down by the lake," he said.

"Great choice. I love you! Keep in touch!" I called as he headed off.

As soon as he hit the door, I ran upstairs and out onto the little balcony off the game room. It provides a clear view of the old tree. Good, that would help me for a while. But I had yet to come up with a strategy to keep Christian in sight when he moved on from there. I decided I would take the dogs for a walk and trail him. If he spotted me, I would just look surprised and say, "Gosh, I'm so sorry. I had no idea this was north!"

I watched as Christian sat down on the blanket and got out one of his books. Although he now considers himself "grown," he still seemed like such a little boy to me. Watching him, my heart ached thinking of the day he really will head "north" into adult life.

About fifteen minutes later, he started to pack up his things. I watched to see which way he would head, ready to take off after him at the speed of sound. He stood for a few moments looking to his right and then to his left—apparently north is not as easy to determine as one would assume. He picked up his backpack. He put it back down . . . and picked it up again. Then I realized he was heading home. I ran downstairs and was elbow deep in soapy water by the time he came through the back door.

"Welcome home!" I said.

He walked past me, muttering, "Good times, good times." (For the uninitiated, that's a line made popular by Billy Ray Cyrus on the Disney kids' show *Hannah Montana*).

That night when the dogs had their blanket back and Christian was tucked in his own bed, I asked him how the adventure had been for him.

He said, "I had a good time, Mom. But I would have enjoyed myself more if my bag wasn't so heavy."

CAST YOUR CARES ON HIM

I thought about Christian's comment for a while that night—and have since. I've wonder how many of us are weighed down by the stuff we drag around, day after day, until our baggage hampers our enjoyment of the journey. Even more, I've wonder why we let it happen. Baggage is inevitable; who among us can walk through life without picking up some shame or fears or insecurities, right? The question is, why do we persist in hanging on to these things, jealously guarding our junk as though it's worth keeping?

Scripture reminds us to cast our cares on our Father because he loves us and he won't let his children buckle under the load (Psalm 55:22; 1 Peter 5:7). But even though we have God's open invitation to unpack our heavy bags, we seem to find that very hard to do. We'd rather cart the weight around than take God up on his offer.

A few weeks after Christian's experiment, I was speaking at a church one Sunday morning and I posed two questions:

1. What would it look like if we came through these doors this morning with all our "baggage" visible?

2. Why would we drag our baggage back home with us again instead of unloading it in prayer?

I stayed around for a while at the end of the service to be available to talk. Here are a few of the answers people gave:

- "I don't have time to pray."

- "I'm too tired to pray."

⇢ "I start all right, but then I get distracted."

⇢ "To be honest, I'm not sure God is listening."

I empathize with those concerns, yet I am convinced it would revolutionize our lives if we were better able to understand that prayer is a gift, rather than a chore. Something to look forward to, rather than something we're graded on. It's not about how well we pray, but about Who is listening to our prayers.

WHY DON'T WE PRAY?

So my question is this: if prayer is God's gift to us to help us live on this broken planet, why do we find it so hard to pray? Let's look at some of the thoughts shared by the congregation that Sunday morning.

Too Busy

Saying we don't have time to pray indicates everything else that devours the hours in any given day is more important or more significant than prayer. We might not believe that's true, but we *live* as if it's true. Let me give you an example.

I know that nothing will impact my son's life more than prayer. God designed him and knows him inside and out. He knows the things Christian tells his dad and me and the things he keeps tucked away in his own heart. He knows where Christian will fall down and how he will rise up. He understands Christian's hopes and dreams and his fears and insecurities.

I don't always see those things as clearly as God, of course, but that doesn't mean I'm not to be attentive to them. To the contrary, one of the most important parts of my role as a parent is, of course, to pray for God's hand in Christian's life. But if I look at how I divide up the time I spend on Christian, most of it is on the "doing" side of things as opposed to interceding on his behalf before the throne of grace. I'm not trying to be unrealistic here or beat myself up as an ungodly mother. It's a fact there are things that have to be done each day. Christian needs to be fed, have clean clothes for school, and a home to live in that doesn't look like Attila the Hun just marched his troops through it. I pray for him on the way to school and after I drop him off, and we pray together at night, and until recently I've felt that fulfilled my prayer duty.

As I wrote this book, however, I became aware that my beliefs don't match my behavior. If I honestly believe that the greatest gift I could ever give my son is intentional time devoted to prayer on his behalf, that should take precedence over a multitude of other things that don't really matter.

For instance, as Christmas 2006 approached, I knew Christian really hoped to get the new Nintendo Wii game system. I also knew that very few units would be available. I spent hours going from store to store finding out when each place was expecting their delivery and how many units they had been promised. I knew if he woke up on Christmas morning and the Wii was not waiting for him, he would be disappointed.

Upon reflection, I see there was an urgency to my gift buying that is often missing from my prayer life. The Wii is a game system that will keep his interest at best for a couple of years, as opposed to prayers that could impact his eternal destiny.

Even more important, when I don't consciously carve out significant time to pray for Christian, I carry the burden of not only my own needs but whatever might be going on in his young life too. Rather than allow Jesus to shoulder our cares, I heft them along day after day, depleting the energy I could devote to other things on our behalf.

Think about your own life for a moment. Whether you are a stay-at-home mom or a working mom or not a mom at all, whether you're married or single or young or retired, there are a million and one demands made of you. As women, others naturally look to us to hold everything together and create an atmosphere of peace and love. That's a lot for any one woman to do alone, isn't it?

We don't have to. Christ offers to exchange our heavy loads for a custom-designed one that's much lighter. There's no excuse—not even busyness. The return is just too important.

Too Tired

I don't know about you, but I often find myself at the end of the day thinking (once again), *Where did today go?* By the time Christian finishes his homework and we eat dinner, clean up, walk the dogs, take baths, put in one more load of laundry that I swear I just washed yesterday, and get Christian settled, the day is done—and frankly, so am I! The weight and wear of life have drained every ounce of strength from me.

That kind of exhaustion was certainly true of Jesus' disciples when he needed them the most:

Then Jesus came with them to a place called Gethsemane, and said to the disciples, "Sit here while I go and pray over there." And He took with Him Peter and the two sons of Zebedee, and He began to be sorrowful and deeply distressed. Then He said to them, "My soul is exceedingly sorrowful, even to death. Stay here and watch with Me." He went a little farther and fell on His face, and prayed, saying, "O My Father, if it is possible, let this cup pass from Me; nevertheless, not as I will, but as You will." Then He came to the disciples and found them sleeping, and said to Peter, "What? Could you not watch with Me one hour? Watch and pray, lest you enter into temptation. The spirit indeed is willing, but the flesh is weak." (Matthew 26:36–41 NKJV)

There is no doubt Peter loved Jesus and was devoted to him, but Peter was also clothed in human flesh like you and me. I'm sure he agonized when Jesus woke him later that night. Imagine how Peter felt when he saw Jesus' tear-stained face and realized he had fallen asleep instead of obediently watching and praying.

Scripture explains that there is a war between our spirit and our flesh, between wanting to do more and wanting to take five before doing it. Of course, we often bring it upon ourselves by doing too much. (Reread the previous section if you've already forgotten!) The apostle Paul describes this battle between spirit and flesh in Romans 7. He writes, "Why don't I do the thing I want to do but instead do the thing I don't want to do?" (v. 15, my paraphrase). I'm sure Paul knew that when we relegate prayer to the bottom of our priority list, we won't have enough energy left to do more than mutter a few familiar phrases before we call it a day.

So we have to consciously work toward increasing our strength for prayer. Christ modeled for us how to live on this earth with all its joys and challenges, and he urged us to watch how he did it. When Jesus' friends asked him to teach them how to pray, he gave them—and us—a pattern to follow:

> In this manner, therefore, pray: Our Father in heaven, hallowed be Your name. Your kingdom come. Your will be done on earth as it is in heaven. Give us this day our daily bread. And forgive us our debts, as we forgive our debtors. And do not lead us into temptation, but deliver us from the evil one. For Yours is the kingdom and the power and the glory forever. Amen. (Matthew 6:9–13 NKJV)

This prayer is not something to rattle off at the end of a busy day. In Christ's model prayer, we begin the day worshipping God and asking for bread for that day. We ask for physical provision, acknowledging that whether we are in good times or bad, everything we have comes from God. We ask for strength and grace and courage for everything we will face that day. We don't know what that will be, but our Father does. We ask for forgiveness and the grace to forgive and for protection from the evil one.

What a wonderful way to begin each and every day. I encourage you to fight the "I'm too tired to pray" blahs with Christ's model prayer. Then, by nightfall, when you're ready to hit the hay, your prayers can be ones of thanksgiving from a grateful heart.

Too Distracted

It's important to remember that we have an enemy who doesn't want us to pray. He knows how effective prayer is, so he is continually devising ways to tempt us to forget to pray. As Guy King writes in his book *Prayer Secrets*: "No one is a firmer believer in the power of prayer than the devil; not that he practices it, but he suffers from it."[1]

I think it's easy to get so caught up in the physical challenges of our days that we forget the very real spiritual battle that rages on around us. We have an enemy who hates God and all God loves. In *The Screwtape Letters*, C. S. Lewis powerfully describes how Satan views humanity versus how God views us. Screwtape, a senior devil, writes to his nephew, Wormwood, a junior devil: "We want cattle who can finally become food; He wants servants who can finally become sons [and daughters]."[2] Our enemy would love to keep us so distracted and busy that we forget to focus on what really matters: our relationship with our Father. Family, work, friends, even church—if we're not careful, all these things can end up robbing us of the joy of being children of God.

Jesus knew this. The gospel writers record moments when Jesus purposely pulled away, not only from the crowds, but even from his friends, to be able to be alone with his Father, often through the whole night. He obviously craved that time to restore himself.

Of course, not all of us are refreshed by being alone the way Jesus was. Each of us has a unique, God-given personality that affects how easily we're distracted and by what, what helps us refocus and what doesn't. Barry finds it hard to believe I can take my laptop to my favorite coffee shop and write for hours no matter how noisy it is. I find it easy because it's not my noise; if I don't know the people milling around me, I can focus on what I'm doing. But if I'm at home, the minute one dog jumps off the sofa I am immediately thinking something like, *If that little monkey goes back into the fireplace . . . !*

You might be able to focus well in your own kitchen or as you wait in the carpool lane or for the elevator at work. What matters is finding a place where you know you can block out other distractions and enjoy being with the Father, who longs to spend time with you. Even more important is making the commitment to fight our human tendency toward distraction. Sometimes I will take a notebook and write down twenty things that I love about being God's daughter. I think of what it means to me when Christian tells me what he loves about me, so I can only imagine that our specific declarations of love to God are precious to him.

One of my latest additions to my daily schedule is to go out into the backyard first thing every morning and say, "Good morning, Father. Thank you that you love me today and that nothing that happens to or through me will be a surprise to you. Father me through this day."

Remember, the enemy is actively seeking to keep us from our appointed prayer tasks. It's one thing to have a prayer closet and another to consciously choose to use it each and every day. The same God who raised Jesus from the dead waits for you there—what an invitation!

Not Sure God Is Listening

Sometimes we find it difficult to pray because we're not sure God is listening to us. That's what a man—he looked to be in his forties, successful, married with children—once said to me. When I asked him why he thought God might not be listening, he said he could see no evidence of God having heard him. He told me he has been in the church most of his life but recently has found himself wondering if anything he believed was actually true.

To be honest, he's not alone. I hear similar concerns in many e-mails and letters I receive:

- "What if I'm just fooling myself into believing that God is really listening?"

- "What proof do I have that my prayer makes any difference at all?"

- "With everything that's going on in the world, why would God care about my concerns?"

- "I think God listens to some people and not to others."

- "I don't think I'm one of God's 'special' ones."

- "If God is really listening, shouldn't I be able to feel his presence?"

I think one of our greatest challenges in prayer is *feeling* God's presence. We live in a sensory age where we are bombarded by ads for quick fixes and miracle drugs that claim to make us feel better and look better. The discipline of prayer offers no easy solutions for the wounds and worries of life, and it often goes without physical sensation. It's therefore tempting to believe prayer isn't worth the time.

But prayer isn't supposed to offer a simple solution. It's meant to be a place to take our concerns and lay them at Jesus' feet. When we approach our petitions in that way, they become not just a time to test God's response but an opportunity to release the cares of our lives.

THE DOOR IN THE WALL

Yes, it is hard to pray. It's much easier to spend our free time flopping down and turning on the television than following the example of Christ and pulling away from the noise and distractions for alone time with our Father. Every believer has experienced the difficulties of an intentional prayer life. But when we persist in seeing prayer as a challenge—as a wall between us and God—and walk away in defeat, we walk away carrying the same burdens we arrived with.

Instead, we need to imagine that there's a door in that wall, like C. S. Lewis's wonderful wardrobe that took Lucy into Narnia in *The Lion, the Witch and the Wardrobe*. Prayer is our escape from this world. As I said earlier, prayer is not a chore or something we'll be tested on at the end of each week. It's our time to crawl into our Father's embrace and lay our cares upon him. Jesus told us that in this world we will have many troubles, but not to be afraid because he has overcome this world (John 16:33). It's only when we are able to quiet the noises outside and within that we remember all his amazing promises to us.

Prayer is not something that belongs on our to-do list, but rather on our to-live list! It would be sad if, when we finally stand before the Lord and he asks us, "Did you enjoy the journey?" we say, "I did, but I would have enjoyed it better if my bags weren't so heavy."

O God, give Thou ear to my plea,
And hide not Thyself from my cry;
O hearken and answer Thou me,
As restless and weary I sigh.

O that I had wings like a dove,
For then I would fly far away
And seek for the rest that I love,
Where trouble no more could dismay.

Nay, soul, call on God all the day;
The Lord for thy help will appear;
At eve, morn, and noon humbly pray,
And He thy petition will hear.

Thy burden now cast on the Lord,
And He shall thy weakness sustain;
The righteous who trust in His Word
Unmoved shall forever remain.

—PARAPHRASE OF PSALM 55, AUTHOR UNKNOWN

4

Do My Prayers Make a Difference?

If God Has Already Decided What He Is Going to Do, Why Pray at All?

The trouble with our praying is, we just do it as a means of last resort. —WILL ROGERS

The world is full of so-called prayer warriors who are prayer-ignorant. They're full of formulas and programs and advice, peddling techniques for getting what you want from God. Don't fall for that nonsense. This is your Father you are dealing with, and he knows better than you what you need. —MATTHEW 6:7–8 MSG

In 1872, geographer, explorer, and statistician Francis Galton conducted a research project to see if he could mathematically prove whether prayer worked or not. His theory was simple: if prayer works, then the British royal family should live longer than any of their subjects, as they were prayed for regularly in churches and homes across the British Isles. However, when he compared the royal family's longevity with that of the general public, he found no difference. He therefore concluded he had proven prayer does not work. (He did not, however, investigate the dietary habits of Queen Victoria or Prince Albert!)

How would Galton fit into today's world? Well, if you ask people in the United States if they believe in prayer, I think the majority of us would say we do. The great divide would come in how we define prayer, why we pray, and who we believe we are praying to.

One of my cousins, Jackie, landed in Francis Galton's camp. Lack of physical results convinced her that prayer was a complete waste of time.

It happened years ago during a visit from Jackie and her sister, Maureen. Our house was fairly small, so my brother, Stephen, surrendered his room to them with quite a detailed list of what not to touch. You might think that's a bit extreme, but Stephen was very careful with his things, and Maureen and Jackie were famous for touching things they shouldn't. I should know—I caught Jackie redhanded with one item. Jackie was fascinated with Stephen's globe, and no matter how many times she was told to leave it alone, the temptation was too much for her. One morning I caught her with it. Her response? She looked at the globe and very indignantly announced, "This thing is in my bed again!"

So you can understand my mom's prudence when she unplugged the bedside lamp. She was afraid the girls would hurt themselves because of their fascination with unscrewing anything that could be unscrewed.

Sticky fingers aside, we had a lot of fun with our cousins. But it was Jackie's question about prayer that really cracked me up. She and Maureen had not been taught to say prayers at night, so my mom taught them a simple prayer we used often:

Jesus, gentle shepherd, hear me.
Bless thy little lamb tonight.
Through the darkness, be thou near me.
Keep me safe till morning light.

One night Jackie said to Mom, "I don't know why we keep saying that prayer, because it doesn't work."

Mom asked her what she meant; did she not feel safe with us?

"It's not that," Jackie said. "It's just that we've prayed for that lamp"—she pointed at the bedside table—"now for three nights, and it's still not working!"

Since Mom had unplugged the lamp, it, of course, wasn't working. More important, since Jackie had taken the prayer literally (incorrect pronunciation of *lamb* aside), her expectations were obviously not met.

Though this story is humorous, Jackie's question about prayer is very serious. Why bother? Why pray? If God knows everything and has already planned what will happen in life, then what difference do our prayers make? Is prayer just an exercise to please God, like learning calculus in school when we hope we will never, by the grace of God, use it again? Is it simply a behavior that identifies us as Christians?

GOING THROUGH THE MOTIONS

The scribes and Pharisees certainly believed the appearance of religion was key to faith. That's one of the reasons they had such a hard time with Jesus and his friends—the disciples did not fit their traditional religious mold. For religious leaders in the days of

Christ, spirituality was based on your physical demeanor. To their mind, a strong prayer life was characterized by loud wailings and cries to God or a pitiful demeanor broadcasting to the world that, yes, they were fasting . . . again! Therefore, to the scribes and Pharisees, the laughter and boisterous habits of Jesus' disciples demonstrated their lack of spirituality.

Jesus, as we know, thought differently. He saw in his disciples the promise of joyful and healthy prayer lives—even in the disciples others would consider incapable of such faith. Take Matthew, a tax collector.

Now, before I go further, remember that although the very mention of the IRS may bring a shudder to many of us today, it is nothing compared to how tax collectors were thought of in Israel at the time of Christ. They were viewed as cruel, ruthless, and predatory. So much so that when Jesus gave his famous Sermon on the Mount, he used tax collectors to deliver a powerful verbal punch: "If you love those who love you, what reward will you get? Are not even the tax collectors doing that?" (Matthew 5:46). The implication was clear: if you believe demonstrating your love for those who love you is an indication of faith, then consider that even those you despise can do that. (Obviously tax collectors were on par with, say, pond scum.)

But Jesus looked at Matthew and, as only he can do, saw beyond the job description to his heart. He invited Matthew to leave his old life and follow him. And in his excitement, Matthew threw a lavish party. It was quite a mixed bunch who attended; alongside the Pharisees and teachers of the law, Matthew invited a lot of his friends . . . who happened to be tax collectors. I imagine Matthew wanted his tax collector friends to meet the man who had changed his life, but you can imagine the distain that radiated from the religious leaders in the room—and where they placed the blame.

In the midst of the party, the Pharisees asked Jesus an important question: "Why do you eat and drink with tax collectors and 'sinners'? . . . John's disciples often fast and pray, and so do the disciples of the Pharisees, but yours go on eating and drinking" (Luke 5:30, 33).

Their criticism of Jesus was clear:

⇢ "Your friends do not look very godly. If you are who you say you are, you wouldn't be hanging with a crowd like this."

⇢ "We can tell by external appearances which people are close to God. If you 'look' holy, we will assume you are holy, and if you 'look' like a sinner, we will assume you are one."

It's obvious that to the religious leaders, prayer was first and foremost a behavior to impress God and man. It was important to show others how "spiritual" a person was.

If that's what prayer was really all about, then no wonder people would question why they should bother! But as we know, Jesus told the Pharisees he had come to show a new way to live: to love and to pray. And prayer was not to be an external ritual that could be crossed off one's to-do list—but an internal revolution. Just as they wouldn't pour new wine into old, rotting wineskins, they could not pour Jesus' new life into old habits.

As you can imagine, the Pharisees and religious leaders were not pleased with Jesus' declaration. They were happy with things just as they were—because that's the way it had always been.

If you're like me, you've run up against that kind of attitude before. When I was ten years old, I was in a Brownies troop. (If you remember, Brownies are the first level of Girl Scouts. Although the group is slightly different than in the States, Brownies are very popular in Scotland.) I loved it. We were split into four groups: the Fairies, the Daisies, the Sprites, and the Kelpies. I was glad I was a Kelpie, as the Fairies had to do way too much skipping, in my opinion. The Kelpies—based on an old Scottish folktale of a horse that could dive under water—were much more adventurous to me.

I enjoyed all of the badge work associated with being a Brownie —except for semaphore, which was compulsory. Semaphore is a type of sign language using large arm motions that can be spotted at a distance (sort of like when you're trying to reach your husband in electronics while you're in the middle of the perfume section in a department store). I hated it. Apart from the fact that it was difficult to learn, I felt like a total idiot doing it. A ten-year-old girl in a Brownie uniform looking as if she is trying to land an airplane in the middle of Ayr Baptist Church lower hall is not a sight I ever want to see again.

But when I complained to Miss Chris, our troop leader, she told me I had to learn it. Why? Because "It's what makes you look like a Brownie!"

That's the way many people in the time of Christ (and today too) considered prayer—it's something that makes you "look" like a devout follower of God. (Some of the Pharisees were so devout they were known as the "bleeding Pharisees." They would pray with their eyes to heaven and therefore kept walking into walls and falling over passing goats!) To them, prayer had nothing to do with an actual relationship with God. It was religious semaphore—posturing for their neighbors.

SOMETHING MORE TO PRAYER

So, is that the way we should look at prayer? Just going through the motions? Believing that if God already knows the end from the beginning, then prayer is nothing more than an external ritual?

Or is there something to Jesus' proclamation of prayer having an internal and eternal purpose?

Most emphatically, yes! While at times it might seem to us as though we're praying by rote, parroting words we've been told are "correct," prayer is much more. Prayer is our perfect means of communication with our Creator. That in and of itself is reason enough for us to pray, isn't it?

Let's take a look at a few of the benefits of praying.

All About Trust

I believe one of the reasons it is important for us to talk to God is that prayer implies trust. It's our way of saying to God:

⋅❯ "I believe you are in control."

⋅❯ "I believe you love me."

⋅❯ "I believe you make everything work out for good no matter how things may appear."

The first words of the prayer Jesus taught his followers were, "Our Father." The picture is a very intimate one—an invitation to come as a child and curl up on your father's lap and tell him all about it.

I've heard Donald Miller speak of the way believers often approach God as if he were their boss, apologizing for being late or not quite "on task." He reminded us of Christ's welcome to pray to "Our Father" and asked, "When was the last time you curled up in your boss's arms and shared your heart?"

Avoiding the obvious bad jokes, Miller's point is clear. We are invited into a relationship of absolute trust and draw close to our Father's heart. The more time we spend in God's presence, the more our trust grows even when things don't go as we planned.

In the spring of 2006, Barry and I did a very foolish thing. We bought a new house before our other house sold. I have counseled people against doing this kind of thing, but it's amazing how blind we can be when we see what we want before our eyes. We were in quite a noisy neighborhood where teenagers in their cars raced down the same streets my son wanted to ride his bike or skateboard on. Additionally, some kids in the local high school discovered who I was, what I do most weekends, and where I lived and were beginning to make quite a nuisance of themselves showing up at all hours with ridiculous questions:

"Do you know Amy Grant?"

"Can you get us good seats for the U2 tour?"

"Do you need a backing band?"

Two of them rang the doorbell one night selling magazines for a school trip. I was happy to support them and went to get my purse. But instead of waiting at the front door, they came inside and into the kitchen, where they informed me that I was—wait for it—"hot"! I nearly choked as I told them I was old enough to be their mother. That didn't seem to put them off at all, and they wanted to know if Barry traveled at all and left me by myself.

I kicked them out, but the experience really shook me up. So Barry and I decided to look for a home in a quieter, gated community. We found one we really liked. It had a nice yard for the dogs and was close to several of Christian's friends from school. We put our house on the market, but it just sat there for a while. And then the builder of the new house told us there was quite a bit of interest in his home and if we wanted it we should move on it. (Yes, I know builders always say that.)

We talked to someone at our bank and decided to go ahead, believing that the other house would surely sell in the summer. Yet summer came and went, as did fall. I felt sick that we had put ourselves in such a vulnerable position.

I didn't even know how to pray. How could I ask God to help us sell a house when there were children dying of starvation around the world without a blanket to cover them? How could I ask for help when it was our foolishness that had put us in this place?

As I write, the house still has not sold. What I am learning through this process, though, is that I have a Father who welcomes me with open arms in the good days and bad days of life. He is here when I make good choices or bad choices. My assurance as the weeks passed was not that he was going to suddenly give some poor, unsuspecting soul a compulsion to buy our house, but rather that whatever happened, he was with us.

Prayer forges within us a deep awareness of God's trustworthiness. He wants us to trust him. He also wants us to love him.

All About Love

Prayer is a way for us to experience love. And not just us showing our love for God, but *receiving* love from God!

When I was twenty-five years old, British pop star Cliff Richard produced an album for me using his band members. One of Cliff's guitar players was a shy, sweet man named Terry Britton. Terry was also a songwriter, and one day he played a little bit of a song he had just written. I'm sure Terry had no way of knowing when he sat down with his trusty guitar that this song—"What's Love Got to Do with It?"—would be recorded by Tina Turner and go straight to number one on the Billboard charts. As I think about the title of that song and our question on the relevancy of prayer, it would seem clear to me that love has *everything* to do with it. The more in love we are with the Father and with our Savior, Jesus, the more we become like him. Couples who have been married for a long time say that they know each other so well they can complete the other's sentences. Imagine having that same relationship with God—to communicate with him so intimately and often. Imagine the benefits of such a relationship—the outpouring of love.

God longs to share his heart with us. He is not looking for perfect little robots to follow directions but people who will share his love. I think it's very difficult for us to embrace the love of God because we have never been loved that way before. That's because all human love—even the best we have experienced—is conditional and is impacted by our behavior or changing circumstances. But God's love is not.

Every time I take a trip home to Scotland, one of the first places I visit is a ruined castle that stands on the edge of a cliff over the ocean. I look at what man had built (the castle) and how time has eroded the stone. Then I look at the ocean, which continues to tumble over the rocks and into the shore in season and out. And I think of how the love God has for us is vast like the ocean. It is not beaten or diminished by time. It is constant, strong, and eternal.

All About Change

Finally, an important reason for prayer is that it can effect change—even in God's plan.

"What?" you say. "My prayers can change the course of God's plan? But . . . he's God!" Well, yes, that's true. But it's also true that on occasion God has listened to the petitions of his people and deliberately chosen to change his plan. Not always. But sometimes.

Take a look at God's relationship with the people of Israel as charted through the pages of the Old Testament. It's heartbreaking. No matter how many times he rescued the Israelites from enemies, starvation, and ruin, each time they turned away from him and forgot who they were. Perhaps the most grievous occasion happened when Moses was receiving the Ten Commandments from God on Mount Sinai. As far as the Israelites were concerned, Moses was taking too long. So they melted all their gold jewelry, shaped it into an image of a calf, and began to worship it.

God was furious at the idolatrous Israelites and determined to disown and destroy them. "And the LORD said to Moses, 'Go, get down! For *your people* whom you brought out of the land of Egypt have corrupted themselves'" (Exodus 32:7 NKJV; emphasis added). Notice that God no longer called the Israelites "my people." He now refers to them as "your people"—they now belonged to Moses. God showed his servant how his heart was broken by this flagrant, intentional betrayal. He told Moses to leave him alone to burn in his wrath and then he would wipe out the Israelites and start again by creating a new nation from Moses.

Here's where it gets interesting. Moses begged God to reconsider. He asked God how it would appear to the Egyptians that the

God of Israel had delivered his people only to slaughter them on a mountain. He prayed,

> Stop your anger. Think twice about bringing evil against your people! Think of Abraham, Isaac, and Israel, your servants to whom you gave your word, telling them "I will give you many children, as many as the stars in the sky, and I'll give this land to your children as their land forever." And God did think twice. He decided not to do the evil he had threatened against his people. (Exodus 32:12–14 MSG)

What a fascinating dialogue. It's almost as if Moses was reminding God who he is. The key has to be that Moses shared God's heart for his people. Moses recalled to God the vision God has always had for his people. This was not a "God, please bless my project" prayer but rather a "God, let's remember *your* project" prayer.

And God changed his mind. Unbelievably, he heeded Moses' words and allowed his flawed and ignorant people to continue so that they might learn.

Lest you think this was a one-time thing, there are several other examples in the Bible of God changing his mind. Take Genesis 18, where we read that God determined to destroy the city of Sodom. Abraham asked God if he would change his mind if there were fifty righteous people there, and God agreed.

Abraham, realizing he might have overestimated the number of righteous citizens, kept reducing the number—forty-five, forty, thirty-five, thirty, twenty, and, finally, ten. Each time God was willing to change his mind, even to the point of saying if there were only ten righteous in the whole city it would be spared.

The sad reality was that the final estimate was still too high, and God did end up destroying Sodom. But the amazing thing about this story is that God was willing to listen to one of his servants and change his intent based on his cry for mercy. In this—and the other situations—he was turned by love and mercy, moved by the cry of a faithful man such as Moses or Abraham, or the repentance of an entire nation as in Nineveh.

Imagine, then, the possibilities for us. There are so many things in this world we can pray for—so many things to ask God to intervene in and change the course of our future. It may not be an answer we see in our lifetime or even ten lifetimes. But unless we pray, we cannot hope for anything different.

PRAYER MAKES A DIFFERENCE IN US

So once again, let's look at the question: if God has already decided the future, does prayer make a difference? The answer is yes. Prayer makes a difference in *us*. And although it might not make a difference *in* our unchanging God, it is a gift *to* him. When used properly, as something more than a ritual, prayer allows us to communicate with God and be reminded of his love and his plan for us. How would it impact your life if you walked around every day with a deep awareness of being overwhelmingly loved? God wants people who will share his heart and work with him for things that have eternal worth, not simply people who place value on the words of the moment. If we can look at prayer that way, there's no way we can doubt the difference it makes in our lives.

And yet we can't help but get discouraged when we are desperate for God to act and heaven seems silent—when even though we want to share his heart, he appears not to see that ours is broken.

There's a wideness in God's mercy,
Like the wideness of the sea;
There's a kindness in His justice,
Which is more than liberty.

There is no place where earth's sorrows
Are more felt than up in Heaven;
There is no place where earth's failings
Have such kindly judgment given.

There is welcome for the sinner,
And more graces for the good;
There is mercy with the Savior;
There is healing in His blood.

There is grace enough for thousands
Of new worlds as great as this;
There is room for fresh creations
In that upper home of bliss.

For the love of God is broader
Than the measure of our mind;
And the heart of the Eternal
Is most wonderfully kind.
—FREDERICK W. FABER

part 2

the
problem

5

Why Does God Say No?

*If God Is Loving and Kind, Why Doesn't
He Give Me What I Want?*

I still pray but it's something automatic, and I'm not even sure I still
believe in it. . . . Because I've suffered, and God didn't listen to my
prayers. —PAULO COELHO, BRAZILIAN AUTHOR

And He was withdrawn from them about a stone's throw, and He knelt
down and prayed, saying, "Father, if it is Your will, take this cup away from
Me; nevertheless not My will, but Yours, be done." Then an angel appeared
to Him from heaven, strengthening Him. And being in agony, He prayed
more earnestly. Then His sweat became like great drops of blood falling
down to the ground. —LUKE 22:41–44 NKJV

Nothing challenges our faith more than when we feel as if God is
indifferent to our cries for help. As I look back down the path of my
own life, various faces and stories come to mind. Even as I reflect on
them now, I remember the pain and the questions, the faith, the
pleading, and the tears. One of them hit very close to home.

When my mother-in-law, Eleanor, was diagnosed with inoperable cancer, she took the news much better than her husband, William, or her son, Barry. William was understandably devastated at the thought of losing his closest companion and wife of many years. But Barry was even more traumatized. You see, Barry has lost many family members to cancer over the years—something that has tinged his life with a dread that exceeds what most of us experience when faced with the disease. To him the thought was terrifying.

Eleanor was much more matter-of-fact about the diagnosis. She wanted a second opinion, so she and William drove to Nashville, where Barry and I lived at the time, to be seen by a cancer specialist at Vanderbilt Hospital. Neither William nor Barry wanted to go with her, so I accompanied Eleanor to her appointment.

The kind doctor listened to her concerns and answered her questions. After he reviewed her test results, he came back into the room and sat down. Eleanor said to him, "I would like you to give it to me straight. I want to know the whole truth."

He honored her request and said, "The cancer has spread from your colon to your liver. I estimate that you should have between six months to two years, depending on what course of treatment you pursue."

And so it began.

Neither of us said anything on the elevator ride down to the hospital lobby. Once we were in the car, I asked Eleanor if she wanted to go straight home or stop somewhere for coffee. She opted for the latter. As we both sat nursing our cups, I asked her, "How are you doing with this news?"

"It's pretty much what I expected," she said. "But somehow it seemed so cold and clinical. It felt as if he were talking about someone else."

I understood exactly what she meant. One moment she was fine and her biggest complaint was that the lawn needed a good downpour of rain—and the next moment she was given an hourglass with the sands of her life moving rapidly through it.

We drove home and told William and Barry what the doctor said. My heart ached for all three of them as over the next few days we discussed Eleanor's options before she and William drove back to Charleston. I was pretty sure she was going to proceed with chemotherapy even though the thought of it was overwhelming. The doctor had made it clear if she wanted to fight for two years as opposed to six months, chemo would have to be part of the package.

Over the next couple of weeks, Eleanor came to a couple of decisions, one of which I expected and one I could not have anticipated.

THE LONG JOURNEY

Eleanor decided to take a vigorous course of chemotherapy, which I wholeheartedly supported. It was her desire to buy time for herself. When she was diagnosed, she was just sixty-four years old, and her one and only beloved grandchild, Christian, was only eighteen months. She wanted as much time with Christian as she could get.

Which led to her next decision that caught me a little off guard.

The phone rang one day, and it was Eleanor. We chatted for a few moments and then I told her I would get Barry. But she stopped me.

"It's you I want to talk to," she said.

I was quite surprised. She always rang to talk to Barry or say sweet things to Christian. But not me. Eleanor and I had a . . . *challenging* relationship. She had tried to get pregnant for twelve years, so when Barry was finally born he was greatly treasured by his mom and dad. And when I came into the picture, it was clear to me that I was "the other woman"! Eleanor and I did our best to get along, but our relationship was decidedly strained.

So I was a bit taken aback that she wanted to talk to me.

"What would you think if I started traveling with you as Christian's nanny?" she asked.

I didn't know what to say. As you may know, I am part of the core team of speakers and authors who travel about thirty weekends every year under the banner Women of Faith. Christian and Barry had traveled with me since Christian was just six weeks old. We had a much-loved nanny who traveled with us, but she had just been offered a live-in position she really wanted to take, so I had been looking to replace her. But not with . . . well, you know!

In other words, the thought of being on the road with my mother-in-law didn't automatically fill me with odes of joy.

I asked, "What about your treatment, Mom? What about your chemotherapy schedule?"

"I'll just take the Women of Faith schedule to the doctor and ask him to fit my treatments in around it," she said as if she had it all in place.

"But the travel is really tiring, Mom. All the flights and airports and hotels," I mumbled on.

"Sheila," she said with a quiet dignity in her voice, "if you knew you had less than two years to live, would you want to share them with those you love or sitting around waiting to die?"

There was nothing more to be said. Eleanor and William became Christian's nannies. It was hard at first, especially because I felt guilty over Eleanor's condition. I could tell at times when I got back from the arena that she felt bad, but she kept going. And William was a tremendous help. Through God, I learned to get out of the way and allow love to pour forth wherever it would. And as it turned out, Eleanor and William were wonderful companions for Christian.

As the months went on, though, and Eleanor began to feel the impact of the cancer and the chemotherapy more and more, she began to look for a different answer. She asked me one weekend if she could come to the arena and have dinner with the speakers and join us for prayer. I told her they would all love that. During our prayer time, she began to weep and in a simple, transparent manner told God she was not ready to die. We gathered around her and laid our hands on her and prayed God would have mercy on her and heal her body.

Not long after that she asked me to attend a healing crusade with William and her. It was being led by a well-known preacher—someone I'd met a couple of times while cohost of *The 700 Club*—so I was glad to say yes. It was wonderful to see Eleanor that night, looking confident as she received a prayer full of faith and conviction that she would be healed. I knew she was deeply moved and hopeful that God had answered our petitions. We were all hopeful.

But as the weeks passed, it became clear Eleanor was losing her battle with this ravenous invader. She was soon unable to travel with us anymore, so during the week Charleston became our home. As it got closer to the end, we took turns staying up with her at night. One night she and I had a heartbreaking conversation.

I thought she was asleep. I had called the hospice nurse and asked if I could give her a little more morphine because she was in pain, and she had said yes. Eleanor could no longer swallow pills, so I'd very carefully measured out a little liquid and mixed it with some ginger ale. She now lay quietly.

"If it was you who had cancer, God would have healed you," she whispered.

"What do you mean?"

"Well, you've lived your life for him and you spend all your time doing things for him. He would heal you."

I looked at her with tears rolling down my face. "Mom, God loves you every bit as much as he loves me. Don't you know that?"

"I don't know. I think you're a better person than I am," she said.

"Mom, that's not true. And anyway, God's love for us isn't based on our behavior; it's based on who he is—based on his heart."

"Some of the things I've said to you . . . I didn't mean them." Her face was suddenly as wet as mine.

"Of course I know that," I said. "You're afraid; we say things we don't mean when we're afraid."

"Why do you think God didn't heal me, Sheila?" she whispered, sobbing quietly.

"Oh, Mom, I don't know. I wish I had answers for you, but I don't know. All I do know is that he loves you. That's all I know."

I sat beside her in her hospice bed. As she fell asleep on my shoulder, my tears soaked her lovely red hair.

WHY, LORD?

One of the greatest mysteries—and challenges—of our relationship with God in prayer is knowing he is both loving and powerful. If God were just *loving*, then when our prayers went unanswered we'd make peace with it—telling ourselves if he were powerful he would have intervened. If he were *powerful* but not loving, we would assume him indifferent to our pain.

But that's not who God is. Not only does he love us with a passion that exceeds our understanding, but God is also powerful enough to intervene at any moment and change our circumstances. And sometimes he does do that. But more often, he does not. The question is why?

When Barry and I lived in Nashville, one of the families in our small group at church walked through an absolute nightmare in which they asked that same question.

David and Nancy Guthrie had one son, Matthew, when they gave birth to a beautiful baby girl. They named her Hope. It was immediately clear to them Hope had some challenges. She was clubfooted, and she was very lethargic and couldn't suck. On her second day of life, they were given the devastating news that Hope had Zellweger syndrome. Zellweger syndrome is a rare congenital disorder (present at birth) characterized by a lack of the cell structures that rid the body of toxic substances in the liver, kidneys, and brain. There is no cure, and most infants die at about six months of age.

Hope lived for 199 days.

To have a child with Zellweger syndrome requires that both parents be carriers of the recessive gene for the syndrome. So after Hope was born, David and Nancy took surgical steps to prevent a future pregnancy. And yet, for whatever reason, it didn't work. Just a year and a half after Hope died, Nancy discovered she was pregnant again. And a few months later, prenatal testing revealed the little boy also had the fatal syndrome.

Gabriel lived for only 183 days.

I find it hard to even imagine the pain of burying one child. But the agony of having to live through it twice is immeasurably beyond what I am able to grasp. The test of faith in situations like that is extreme. How do you continue to love and worship the one who could have saved the life of your child and did not? How do you trust the One who, even though you did everything in your power to prevent another pregnancy, allowed you to become pregnant again? And with another child who would live such a brief life?

I cannot speak to that, but Nancy can and did. In her book *Holding on to Hope: A Pathway Through Suffering to the Heart of God,* Nancy wrote about her family, honestly describing their pain and struggle in the midst of grief.[1]

Nancy also told how she and her family determined to move beyond the questions. She related their experiences to Job—bewilderment in the face of such extreme circumstances and yet full of faith that God was with them, loving them, no matter what. In doing so, they were able to understand that just as Job survived, so would they. Even if they didn't understand why God was putting them through that trial.

LONGING AND SURRENDER

Christ also lived through his Father saying no. I have listened to those who try to minimize his agony in the Garden of Gethsemane, saying that as he was fully God and man, Jesus knew the great joy and victory ahead and therefore didn't mind knowing he was soon to die a painful death. I reject that with everything that is in me. Our Savior was fully man, and he suffered as a man would (although without sinning). Jesus knew that he was about to walk into the greatest inferno ever faced by one in human flesh and that this was the plan from the beginning of time to redeem fallen humanity. He knew that his Father would allow him to drink from the cup of his wrath and not deliver him.

But Jesus also knew that even when God was telling him no, he was still with him. His prayer is left as a gift for us, a light in the darkest night: "'Father, if it is Your will, take this cup away from Me; nevertheless not My will, but Yours, be done.' Then an angel appeared to Him from heaven, strengthening Him. And being in agony, He prayed more earnestly" (Luke 22:42 NKJV).

Why does God sometimes say no to our prayers? As I'm sure you realize, I don't have the answer to that question. No one does. But what we do have is the knowledge that when we keep praying—when we move beyond "Why?" to "Be with me, Lord"—we begin to learn more about our faith and our strength in our Father. Confronting God with our *why* becomes being with God in our need. He is there when we need him. Always. He might not answer our prayers as we would like, but he will be there to hold us through the trials.

And with him we can endure.

> *Out of my bondage, sorrow, and night,*
> *Jesus, I come, Jesus, I come;*
> *Into Thy freedom, gladness, and light,*
> *Jesus, I come to Thee;*
> *Out of my sickness, into Thy health,*
> *Out of my want and into Thy wealth,*

Out of my sin and into Thyself,
Jesus, I come to Thee.

Out of my shameful failure and loss,
Jesus, I come, Jesus, I come;
Into the glorious gain of Thy cross,
Jesus, I come to Thee.
Out of earth's sorrows into Thy balm,
Out of life's storms and into Thy calm,
Out of distress to jubilant psalm,
Jesus, I come to Thee.

Out of the fear and dread of the tomb,
Jesus, I come, Jesus, I come;
Into the joy and light of Thy throne,
Jesus, I come to Thee.
Out of the depths of ruin untold,
Into the peace of Thy sheltering fold,
Ever Thy glorious face to behold,
Jesus, I come to Thee.
—WILLIAM T. SLEEPER

6

Is God Angry with Me?

Will God Help Me If I'm the One
Who Got Myself into This Mess?

I can forgive, but I cannot forget, is only another way of saying, I will not forgive.
Forgiveness ought to be like a cancelled note—torn in two, and burned up, so
that it never can be shown against one. —HENRY WARD BEECHER

Then Jonah prayed to his God from the belly of the fish. He prayed: "In trouble,
deep trouble, I prayed to God. He answered me. From the belly of the grave I
cried, 'Help!' You heard my cry. You threw me into ocean's depths, into a watery
grave, with ocean waves, ocean breakers crashing over me. I said, 'I've been
thrown away, thrown out, out of your sight. I'll never again lay eyes on your Holy
Temple.'" —JONAH 2:1–4 MSG

How much do you know about the character Jonah in the Old
Testament? Most of us know the story from Sunday school about
the man who ran away from God and was swallowed by a large
fish (or, more popular with flannel-graph artists, a whale).

There is actually a lot more to Jonah's story, particularly as it
addresses this question: will God hear our prayers if we ourselves

caused the mess we are in? In other words, is it possible God is not answering our prayers because he is angry with us?

One of Christian's friends has a little brother who keeps everyone in his family circle highly entertained with his off-the-cuff comments. He once overheard his brother tell Christian that one of the boys at school had said a curse word. The boy's response: "Well, it's off to hell with him. Do not pass go; do not collect your angel wings!"

What about that? Obviously our little buddy's response was quite harsh. But when we read in the Old Testament about God's anger against a person or a nation, there were often dire consequences. Take Moses. A dear friend of God, he was not allowed to cross over into the Promised Land because instead of striking a rock once as he was instructed from God to do, he struck it twice. Because of that one disobedient action, after wandering in the desert with an ungrateful and mutinous people for forty years, he did not get to put one foot on the promised ground (Numbers 20:6–12).

That may seem so unfair. But we have to understand the reasoning behind it. As we know, God used much of the Old Testament to foretell the birth and life of Jesus. In disobeying God and striking the rock twice, Moses blasphemed the picture of the coming Christ who would be struck once for us. In that light, God's punishment, although not completely understood by us, was just in his eyes. In Peter's first letter, he writes, "For Christ also suffered *once* for sins, the just for the unjust, that He might bring us to God, being put to death in the flesh but made alive by the Spirit" (3:18 NKJV; emphasis added). By striking the rock—the picture of Christ—twice, Moses defiled a holy moment, and for that there was a price to be paid.

And even then I see God's heart and love for Moses, his servant and friend. Although there was a price to be paid for disobeying God, he stayed right by Moses' side. God took him to the top of the mountain and let him see the Promised Land. We don't know what took place between them on that mountain, but it seems to me a very intimate picture of a father lifting his son on his shoulders to get a better look at the view.

When Moses died, we read that God buried him (Deuteronomy 34:6). This is the only time in Scripture that such a burial is recorded. God took care of his friend and laid his body to rest. Even in his anger, God showed mercy and love toward Moses. Before the birth and death of Christ, people lived under the law and the law is pretty clear-cut. But even during this time, when the law epitomized God's scale of justice, he still took care of his friend.

"Well, that was Moses!" you might be tempted to say. "He was one of God's favorites. But I don't have that kind of history with God."

During the last eleven years as I have traveled with Women of Faith, I have talked to many women who have expressed these sentiments. I think in particular of a young woman who stood in line to talk to me at a break. Tears poured down her cheeks as she tried to speak. Finally she was able to tell me that she and her husband had been trying to have a baby for four years with no success.

"I know why," she said. "When I was in college, I got pregnant and had an abortion. I know God is angry at me for killing my baby, and that's why he won't give me another one."

My heart ached for this young woman who genuinely believed God was so angry with her that he would punish her by depriving her of the one thing she cherished above all. She was still living under law as opposed to the grace that comes so freely with Christ.

I reminded her then of one of my favorite texts from John's letters:

> If we claim that we're free of sin, we're only fooling ourselves. A claim like that is errant nonsense. On the other hand, if we admit our sins—make a clean breast of them—he won't let us down; he'll be true to himself. He'll forgive our sins and purge us of all wrong-doing. (1 John:8–9 MSG)

I told her, "You are so aware of this thing you did and you drag it with you every day. The truth is we are all sinners; some of us just forget about it most of the time. God's Word is clear: if we will faithfully confess our sins, God is always faithful to forgive. Always."

As Henry Ward Beecher said, God tears up the note and it is never seen again.

NOT ME, LORD!

In the story of Jonah, we see a God who not only is faithful to forgive but also is limitless with his mercy.

Jonah was a patriot. If he'd been born in the United States, he would have been the one with the flag in his front yard and his voice swelling as he sang patriotic songs on the Fourth of July while red, white, and blue firecrackers burst overhead. His very patriotism, however, blinded him to who God really is and what

God wanted to tell his own people. Jonah didn't understand the warning God was actually giving *Israel* when he told Jonah to tell the people of Nineveh he was going to destroy them—unless they turned from sin, in which case he would save them.

It was one of God's great show-and-tell moments, and the message was clear: if God could show mercy to Israel's greatest enemy, how much more mercy would he show his own people?

But Jonah missed all of that.

I believe this great story has a lot to say to us today about God's mercy, as well as his judgment. At the time God called Jonah to go to Nineveh, Jeroboam was ruling over Israel. Jeroboam was a powerful king, but he did not honor God. A man who allowed the worship of foreign gods and idols, he was just like many of the other kings of Israel who "did what was evil in the sight of the LORD." (See Jeremiah, Judges, 1 and 2 Kings, and 1 and 2 Chronicles for the stories of those many kings of Israel who rebelled against God . . . only to be shown mercy by God.)

Of course, Jonah wasn't thinking about such things in the beginning. He was busy predicting the victories described in 2 Kings won by Jeroboam in restoring Israel's land (2 Kings 14:23–26).

Jonah was so happy to be the bearer of good news concerning his own people, he forgot God is bigger than one nation or one political party. Land was then, as it is today in Israel, of great importance. Through the forty-year reign of King Jeroboam, Israel recaptured much of the land they had lost and became once more the premier power in the Middle East, as they had been during the reign of King Solomon. Assyria was weak, and Israel was strong.

It was at this moment in history that God called his prophet Jonah to go to Nineveh, Assyria's capital city, and tell the people that the God of Israel was going to destroy them unless they repented and changed their ways.

Now you'd think a nationalist like Jonah would jump at the chance of announcing to his sworn enemies they were about to be destroyed. It would be like telling a fiercely proud American veteran he could announce to the terrorists around the world that God was going to destroy them for their evil actions. But Jonah's response is surprising. Instead of setting off north to Nineveh, Jonah boarded a ship heading west for Tarshish, most commonly thought to be in the south of Spain, a long way from Assyria. Why did he do that? His answer—given to God after the people of Nineveh repented and God decided to spare their lives—is an interesting one:

> Jonah was furious. He lost his temper. He yelled at God, "GOD! I knew it—when I was back home, I knew this was going to happen! That's why I ran off to Tarshish! I knew you were sheer grace and mercy, not easily angered, rich in love, and ready at the drop of a hat to turn your plans of punishment into a program of forgiveness!" (Jonah 4:1–2 MSG)

Jonah did not approve of that side of God's character. It made him very angry when God extended grace and forgiveness toward anyone other than the Israelites. He wanted a God of wrath who would punish Israel's enemies and show mercy only to his chosen people. If Jonah had thought God was going to wipe out all the people in Nineveh, he would have been there quicker than two swats of a camel's tail. But he knew there was a chance they might repent, and if they did, he knew God would be full of mercy. Jonah was not willing to be the catalyst for that chain of events, so off he went.

YOU CAN RUN, BUT YOU CAN'T HIDE

God intervened twice to get his reluctant courier back on track. The first event was a life-threatening storm that battered the ship as Jonah crossed the Mediterranean Sea. The storm was so fierce the sailors believed they would all be lost. Being a superstitious people, they assumed they had offended one of their gods so they began throwing things overboard, hoping to appease the offended one.

Despite the sailors' efforts, the storm grew in intensity. In desperation, the captain searched the ship to see if they had missed anything. And there he found Jonah, fast asleep in his bunk. The captain woke Jonah and asked him if he had any idea why they'd found themselves in this life-threatening situation. Jonah told them it was his fault. He had run away from the God of Israel, and their only hope of survival was to throw him overboard.

Now the captain had a dilemma. If Jonah's God really was the one to cause this storm, what would happen to them if they threw his friend into the water? But Jonah assured them it was the only thing to do, so they tossed him overboard.

I imagine at this point Jonah being pulled down further and further under the water. But God was not finished with Jonah. As Jonah fought against the waves, the storm immediately calmed. And then God sent a large fish that swallowed Jonah whole.

From the little we know of his life, Jonah appears to have been a very negative, "glass half empty" type of person—he pouted over just about everything God wanted him to do. I would imagine when he hit the belly of the whale he did so with an all-knowing sigh. Finally he was himself the proof that life is not fair—and therefore he would die and accept his demise as inevitable. Perhaps by that point he even welcomed it.

But never assume anything is hopeless where God is working! Now in the belly of this huge fish, Jonah cried out to God.

From the belly of the grave I cried, "Help!" You heard my cry. You threw me into ocean's depths, into a watery grave, with ocean waves, ocean breakers crashing over me. I said, "I've been thrown away, thrown out, out of your sight. I'll never again lay eyes on your Holy Temple. . . . When my life had almost gone, I remembered the LORD." (Jonah 2:2–4 MSG; v. 7 NCV)

When God determined it was time, he caused Jonah's "water taxi" to spit him up onto dry land and gave him another chance to be the bearer of the heart of God.

Once more God told Jonah to go to Nineveh, and this time he went. Nineveh was a large city with upwards of one hundred and twenty thousand people living there at the time (Jonah 4:11). It would take Jonah three days to walk from one side of the city to the other. When he had walked for one day and was approaching the heart of the city, he began to call out that in forty days, God would destroy Nineveh completely.

The people were horrified and decided to wear rough cloth as a sign of their grief. The king heard about Jonah's proclamation and ordered a total fast of food and water. He told his people, "Who knows? Maybe God will change his mind. Maybe he will stop being angry, and then we will not die" (Jonah 3:9 NCV).

That's exactly what happened—just as Jonah had known it would. When God saw the Ninevites' genuine repentance, he did not destroy them. Now we have one *very* ticked-off prophet. Jonah was unable to celebrate the miracle he had just seen. And he missed the huge message God sent to him via one hundred and twenty thousand people that even when God is angry, his heart is turned once more by honest sorrow.

Having decided someone was going to die, Jonah decided it might as well be him. He sat out in the hot desert sun, baking in the heat. God caused a plant to grow up over him and provide him with some shelter. Jonah liked the plant. He sat in its shade and rehearsed and rearranged his bitter thoughts. Until God caused a worm to eat the plant and it withered and died.

Jonah's first response was, "How could you! How could you kill my lovely plant? I'd even given it a name. I called it Cedric!" (my paraphrase).

God said to Jonah, "You just proved my point!"

You are so concerned for that plant even though you did nothing to make it grow. It appeared one day, and the next day it died. Then shouldn't I show concern for the great city Nineveh, which has more than one hundred twenty thousand people who do not know right from wrong? (Jonah 4:10–11 NCV)

Have you ever met people like that? I have. There are some in the body of Christ who have a hard time loving sinners who are guilty of the things they disapprove of. When I was a teenager, we had a girl in our youth group who lost her way for a while. She began to drink heavily and sleep around. She developed quite a reputation, as one can do quickly in a small town. But after a while she wandered back into one of our youth meetings one night.

Most of us were thrilled to see her. After all, we had been praying this would happen. But there were a few who were determined to make any attempted reentry as difficult as possible. I remember one girl saying, "I hope she doesn't think she can just come back in and we'll all forget about what she's been doing."

I could hardly contain myself I was so mad. "I thought that was the whole point," I said. "I thought this was the place where sinners get to wander back into and be welcomed home with open arms."

Perhaps those who have never extended grace to themselves are unable to extend it to others.

THE CHALLENGE OF FORGIVENESS

God's Word is full of stories of those who messed up and were forgiven by God. Not only forgiven but restored to a place of far greater joy and purpose. Think of the great apostle Paul, who tortured God's people until confronted by Christ on the road to Damascus (Acts 9:1–9). Or the woman caught in adultery and publicly humiliated—Jesus didn't condemn her but told her to go and live differently (John 8:3–11).

When I consider people in Scripture who experienced God's forgiveness, I think especially of the apostle Peter. This rough and tough fisherman who was devoted to Christ took quite a fall when he heard the words, "I don't know this man!" tumble from his own lips. I am sure he beat himself up over the next few brutal hours and days as Jesus was crucified and placed in a tomb. I can't imagine how his betrayal must have weighed on him, particularly as Jesus had told him it would happen and he had denied it so vehemently. I wonder if he remembered what else Jesus told him: "Simon, Simon, Satan has asked to test all of you as a farmer sifts his wheat. I have prayed that you will not lose your faith! Help your brothers be stronger when you come back to me" (Luke 22:31–32 NCV).

What a gift! Not *if* you come back, but *when* you come back. On that glorious Easter morning, the women encountered an angel guarding an empty tomb. The angel said to the women, "Go, tell His disciples—*and Peter*—that He is going before you into Galilee" (Mark 16:7 NKJV; emphasis added).

There was to be no doubt that Peter should know that he was welcomed. If the angel had just told the women to tell "the disciples," I wonder if Peter would have gone with them—after all, he had denied even knowing Jesus; how could he ever be forgiven for that? But God knew Peter's heart, and out of all eleven remaining disciples, Peter was the only one individually named in the invitation.

Have you messed up? Do you wonder if God still hears and cares about you? Perhaps you are ashamed to even face what you have done. It may have been something that caused harm not just to you but to others. You may fear facing the truth and beginning the process of restoration because it seems like such a long path home.

If so, have the faith to remember that with God all things can be made new. Your past is just that. But your future in him is limitless. All God looks for is a desire to begin moving in the right direction, and he will be there. And not just passively but waiting to embrace you. Just say the name of Jesus, and the condemnation of the enemy, who would love to keep you in the belly of the whale for the rest of your life, will have to go. You are loved; you are loved; you are loved!

William Blake wrote, "The Glory of Christianity is, To Conquer by Forgiveness."[1] That means you have to be willing to forgive yourself too. I hope you will see that of all of us who run into the arms of a gracious, forgiving Father this day, you might be the only one individually named on the invitation. Welcome home!

From out the depths I cry, O Lord, to Thee,
Lord, hear my call.
I love Thee, Lord, for Thou dost heed my plea,
Forgiving all.
If Thou dost mark our sins, who then shall stand?
But grace and mercy dwell at Thy right hand.
—THE PSALTER, BASED ON PSALM 130

7

Why Does God Seem Absent when I Pray?

Why Does God Seem Near Sometimes and So Far Away at Others?

All was silent as before—
All silent save the dripping rain.

—HENRY WADSWORTH LONGFELLOW

To you I call, O LORD my Rock; do not turn a deaf ear to me. For if you remain silent, I will be like those who have gone down to the pit. Hear my cry for mercy as I call to you for help, as I lift up my hands toward your Most Holy Place. —PSALM 28:1–2

It has to be one of the loneliest experiences for a believer—to pray and yet feel as if God is a million miles away. I remember such a time in my life. The loneliness and despair were overwhelming. I have written in my book *Honestly* about my struggle with clinical depression and my subsequent hospitalization,[1] but I haven't yet written about the weeks that led up to that time. In many ways they were far more difficult. I was calling out to God from the depths of my heart and hearing nothing. I longed for answers and there were none. I was willing to do anything God showed me to do, but the sky was dark and silent.

It was the summer of 1992. I was cohost of *The 700 Club* and lived in Virginia Beach, where the show went out live daily. My life was very busy. I taped *The 700 Club* five days a week and also my own talk show, *Heart to Heart with Sheila Walsh*. Each Friday at the end of the two shows, which were back-to-back, I would quickly change clothes and head to the airport. Most weekends I'd have a concert somewhere on Friday and Saturday nights and get back to Virginia Beach on Sunday, ready to start all over again on Monday morning. I used to blame my manager for overbooking me, but in retrospect, I think I liked the lack of time to think or be alone. Silence was disturbing to me. Silence and solitude invite us to take a look at what might be going on inside, and I didn't want to do that.

I had never heard of clinical depression. I knew people had "bad days," but as far as an actual illness, I didn't know such a thing existed. If someone had attempted to tell me about clinical depression back then, I would have been very skeptical, particularly in reference to the life of a believer. I'm sure my knee-jerk instinct would have been to quote a verse that seemed to suit the situation.

I was guilty of using the life-giving Word of God as a Band-Aid to cover up a wound. Here are some of the verses that came to mind:

> → "I can do all things through Christ, because he gives me strength" (Philippians 4:13 NCV).

⋅⋗ "But in all these things we have full victory through God who showed his love for us. Yes, I am sure that neither death, nor life, nor angels, nor ruling spirits, nothing now, nothing in the future, no powers, nothing above us, nothing below us, nor anything else in the whole world will ever be able to separate us from the love of God that is in Christ Jesus our Lord" (Romans 8:37–39 NCV).

⋅⋗ "But thanks be to God, who always leads us in victory through Christ. God uses us to spread his knowledge everywhere like a sweet-smelling perfume" (2 Corinthians 2:14 NCV).

Don't get me wrong—these are wonderful words that in most situations are meant to uplift us. But rather than help me, my forced happiness and Scripture quoting was hurting me as I compared it to how I really felt—which was nothing like those verses. Rather than allowing the Word of God to be a light to my dark path, it became a harsh judge of what I was not doing or experiencing. My conscience told me I *should* be able to rise above the despair I felt. I *should* be aware of the love of God. I *should* be victorious. This vicious cycle made me miserable.

I had no idea what was wrong with me. All I knew was I felt overwhelmingly sad all the time. But I was able to hide it from others and carry on with my job.

I hid my sadness because there was no apparent reason for it. If anyone had asked me what was wrong with me, I wouldn't have known what to say. If there had been some obvious, glaring sin in my life, my misery would have made more sense to me.

But I couldn't put my finger on anything other than occasionally being too tired to pray or unable to concentrate when I tried to read my Bible. Certainly not anything I'd expect God to "punish" me for.

Physically I felt as if I was losing ground every day. I couldn't sleep or eat. I had an increasingly difficult time concentrating for any amount of time . . . which is challenging when preparing for two live television shows a day!

I decided it must be an attack of the enemy and so I just had to be strong and resist him; after all, God's Word told me that if I resisted the devil, he would flee from me (James 4:7). But no matter how hard or loud or authoritatively I prayed, the darkness didn't leave.

I did everything I knew to do as a Christian. I asked women I had great respect for to pray for me. I fasted and prayed for twenty-one days. And still the heavens seemed silent to me. At this point I was thirty-four years old. I had been a believer since I was eleven, and this was the first time in twenty-three years I felt as if my prayers were not being answered. Actually, it was worse than that—I felt as if they were not being heard.

THE STORM

As I was driving home from the studio one day, a storm began to build. The sky became a strange shade I had never seen before. It wasn't quite black but more a deep, deep red. Thunder rumbled overhead, and lightning slashed across the sky as if someone had taken a blade to rip the heavens to shreds. Rain battered my car and traffic slowed to a crawl. Just a few cars ahead of me, someone had braked sharply and the car behind them slammed into them, as did the one behind the second vehicle.

Something in me reacted, and I pulled over to the edge of the road and stopped my car. I felt so abandoned. The storm seemed to me a physical representation of my spiritual turmoil: nothing made sense to me anymore. I even wondered if I had caused the storm because somehow God was angry with me. I was lost with no place left to turn.

My mind swirled with questions I couldn't seem to answer:

> *What do you do as a believer when you pray and pray and it seems as if God has stopped listening?* Like someone who throws a stone into a deep pit and never hears it hit bottom, I felt as though I was tossing my prayers out into a darkness that never reached God: "Father, do you hear me? Can you see that I am drowning here? I feel so alone. Please help me!"

> *What do you do when everything that you have ever counted on before no longer seems to work?* I consider myself someone who has always walked the straight and narrow, who does all the "right" things, but now no matter what I did, I was losing ground every day: "Father, please tell me what to do—I am lost. I pray, I read your Word, I fast, but nothing changes. I am so afraid."

> *Where else is there to go?* I literally felt as though there was not one door left open to me, not one glimmer of hope: "Father, if there is any mercy left in your heart for me, then

please take me home. I can't do this anymore; it is too hard, and I am too tired. My life is slipping away."

I had reached a crisis: do something or drown.

That afternoon I called my mom, who still lives in the same small town on the west coast of Scotland where I was raised. I told her what was going on with me and said that I felt as if I had lost my way—or as if God had lost me.

Mom encouraged me to take a long look back down this road I have traveled with God. "Has he ever left you before?" she asked.

I knew that he never had. But this time it *felt* different.

"Sheila, you cannot allow how you feel to rob you of the truth that no matter where you are or what is happening with you, God has promised that he will never leave you. And he can't lie."

I took my mother's words and her promise of prayer and wrapped myself up in them that night as I tried to sleep. I knew I needed to get some help. Dr. Henry Cloud had been a guest on my show a few weeks earlier and had given me his card. I called Dr. Cloud and told him I thought I was losing my mind. He told me I wasn't but that I did indeed need help, and he was happy to arrange for that to happen.

If I had been more aware of the signs of clinical depression at an earlier stage, I know now that I could have been helped by counseling or medication; but I never considered such an option. As far as I was concerned, I could keep all the plates spinning in the air for as long as I needed to. I would have been humiliated to admit that I needed help. My identity was based in what I did rather than who I was, and I was so afraid of failing. My fear kept me imprisoned until my pit was so deep I could not get out by myself.

The following evening I was admitted as a patient in a psychiatric ward, where I stayed for a month. As I began to understand the illness of clinical depression, I also began to enjoy a new relationship with my Father. What's important is that this relationship was based on nothing I brought to the table, but simply based on who God is and his love for me.

I wrote in my journal that first night:

I never knew you lived so close to the floor
But every time I am bowed down
Crushed by this weight of grief
I feel your hand on my head
Your breath on my cheek
Your tears on my neck
You never tell me to pull myself together
To stem the flow of many years
You simply stay by my side
For as long as it takes
So close to the floor

WHY DOES GOD SEEM SO FAR AWAY?

Have you ever been there? Has there been a time when no matter how passionately you prayed, God seemed at best indifferent, if not absent? Perhaps your experience was colored by clinical depression, as mine was. Or perhaps there were other reasons for your separation anxiety with God. Let's take a look at a few other reasons we feel cut off from God.

Our Behavior

There are times in our lives when God withdraws his presence because he wants us to pay attention to the destructive path we are on. God loves us, but he's a holy God and he's not going to indulge us when we're living in a way that contradicts his Word.

I received a letter one day from a woman who wanted to know why God was not answering her prayers. She said she needed guidance, but God did not seem to be listening to her. Then she outlined her situation. She told me she was sleeping with three men, and she wanted God to show her which one was the right one for her.

Once I got over my initial shock, I prayed for wisdom and understanding. I did not know this woman's personal history or how she had been raised. I also realized that cultural dos and don'ts had shifted and that the honest tone of this woman's letter made it clear she didn't think she was doing anything wrong. There are many in our culture who have no background in the church or who have been used or abused as children and have patterned their lives on that. They need grace, acceptance, and kindness from us as God makes their path straight and repaints the picture of what love really is.

When I wrote to her, I thanked her for her honesty. I told her it was God's plan for one man and one woman to join their lives together in marriage and within that union to enjoy every good gift God has provided, including sex.

I told her about a man in the Bible called David, who loved God but really messed up. I reminded her of his prayer after he had sinned with Bathsheba. David is known as a man after God's own heart, yet he had arranged for Bathsheba's husband to be killed in battle so that he could have her. Even though David got what his flesh wanted, his spirit grieved at the separation he now felt between himself and God. His prayer is recorded in Psalm 51:

> God, be merciful to me
> because you are loving.
> Because you are always ready to be merciful,
> wipe out all my wrongs.
> Wash away all my guilt
> and make me clean again.
> I know about my wrongs,
> and I can't forget my sin.
> You are the only one I have sinned against;
> I have done what you say is wrong. . . .
> Create in me a pure heart, God,
> and make my spirit right again.
> Do not send me away from you
> or take your Holy Spirit away from me.
> Give me back the joy of your salvation. . . .
> The sacrifice God wants is a broken spirit.
> God, you will not reject a heart that is broken and sorry for sin.
> (vv. 1–4, 10–12, 16 NCV)

Only when David had repented of his behavior and honestly sought God's forgiveness were the floodgates opened and David washed anew in the presence of his Father.

Please understand: each of our personal situations are different. We all come to God in different ways, asking for repentance in different ways. And although God will always, always forgive us, his response to us comes in different ways. It may be a floodgate as with David; it may be a still, small voice in the night, or a feeling of calm like no other. It may come instantly or over time. It may be that our shame is replaced with peace or even that for some time we walk out the consequences of our choices. But the point is that if we call to him, God will be there. We've all sinned. It's up to us to honestly examine our hearts and make sure we're not allowing our own guilt to keep us from the One who forgives and that sin itself is not standing in the way.

Our Behavior Toward Others

There are other times where our prayers can be hindered not just by how our behavior affects us but by how our behavior affects others. Consider, for instance—and I mention this because it's so common—our behavior in the marriage relationship. When we live with someone day in and day out, we have many opportunities to treat our spouses in a way, shall we say, not quite how God intended. No marriage is perfect; we all understand that. But if we continually disrespect our spouse—for whatever reason—without working things out, we build a wall between not only our spouses and ourselves, but God and ourselves.

Peter knew this when he wrote:

In the same way, you husbands should live with your wives in an understanding way, since they are weaker than you. But show them respect, because God gives them the same blessing he gives you— the grace that gives true life. Do this so that nothing will stop your prayers. (1 Peter 3:7 NCV)

I am assuming it probably goes both ways. In fact, I know it does!

The rule works for any relationship. If you know you've been harboring ill will toward anyone—family, spouse, friend, co-worker, etc.—and "coincidentally" you find your prayer life not what it used to be . . . ask God for the grace to change your heart and attitude.

Our Unforgiveness

In my life, one of the greatest rocks to climb over has been when I am unwilling to forgive. I'm sure I'm not alone in that burden. It's hard to admit we've done wrong and say we're sorry. But often it's even harder to forgive. We sometimes thrive on self-righteousness—knowing we've been wronged and wanting to hold that hurt against another indefinitely instead of letting it go.

To my mind the most amazing declaration from the cross is when Jesus cried out, "Father, forgive them, for they do not know what they are doing" (Luke 23:34). Jesus asked God to forgive his torturers while he was still in physical and spiritual agony, not after he had risen from the dead. He prayed that prayer of forgiveness in the midst of the storm, not when the sun began to remind the earth there are better days ahead. Can you imagine how difficult that must have been?

Forgiveness is hard. It is even more difficult when the person who wronged us is not sorry in the least. But when I listen to Christ's words recorded in Matthew's gospel, it's clear to me that if I want to live freely and lightly, then I need to study how Jesus lived:

Are you tired? Worn out? Burned out on religion? Come to me. Get away with me and you'll recover your life. I'll show you how to take a real rest. Walk with me and work with me—*watch how I do it.* Learn the unforced rhythms of grace. (Matthew 11:28–29 MSG, emphasis added)

During my struggle with depression, someone I cherished as a friend walked away from me because of the choice I made to get help and take medication. Initially I felt wounded, but as can often happen, my wound turned to anger. Every time I tried to pray, I saw the person's face. And with that face before me, my view of God was blocked; my prayers fell at my feet.

This seemed hugely unfair to me! I tried to reason with God that I was not the one who had broken the relationship, but he would have none of it. I had a dilemma. I knew I had to forgive the person, but I had absolutely no desire to do so. So I started where I was. My first prayers were pathetic: "Dear God, I know that I have to forgive, so I choose to do so even though I don't mean a word of this."

For weeks I prayed for this person even though my heart was not in it. But an interesting thing began to happen to me. The more I aligned my will with God's will, the more he began to change my heart. As the weeks turned to months, I found myself praying for this person and really meaning it. It was an amazing experience and one I'm truly grateful for, since it freed me from carrying around the weight of unforgiveness for the rest of my life.

As I have told my son countless times, forgiveness is God's gift to help us live in a world that is not fair. More important, though, is the lesson: the more we allow our anger to fade, the more we center ourselves on forgiveness and God, the more opportunity we have to feel his presence and response to our petition. The boulder of bitterness and resentment rolls from our path, and once again we're in communion with God and his will.

There's no doubt this chapter covers a difficult topic. The reasons for God's seeming distance from us are many, and we've all felt that separation at one time or another. But no matter what, we need to remember this: God is sovereign.

One of the greatest lessons I took from that dark moment of my first night in treatment is that God is always there, no matter how we feel. There will be times in our lives that illness or depression, insecurity or doubt, the enemy of our souls or the enemy that we can be to ourselves will make us doubt God is listening. Our feelings, however, do not change the facts and do not alter the character of God. He *is* with you! Hold on to that truth! In the midst of uncertainty or days when God might seem far off, God is present. No matter what *appears* to be true, we can still praise him in the storm.

> There is a calm for ev'ry storm
> We meet from day to day,
> A hallowed peace that dwells within,
> And smiles the clouds away.
> The star of hope still brightly shines,
> Though wild the breakers roar,
> And in its beams the words we trace,
> Life's dream will soon be o'er.
>
> There is a Friend, a constant Friend,
> Who slumbers not nor sleeps,
> But safe within His tender care
> The trusting soul He keeps;
> His bow of love still spans the sky,
> And points to yonder shore,

While on its beams the words we trace,
Life's cares will soon be o'er.

There is a morn when we shall wake
At home beyond the tide,
And in our Savior's likeness then
We shall be satisfied;
O hearts that yearn and bleed and break
For joys that come no more,
Look up and read the blessèd words,
Life's tears will soon be o'er.

—FANNY CROSBY

8

Why Did God Help Her but Not Me?

Does God Have Favorites?

Whenever a friend succeeds, a little something in me dies. —GORE VIDAL

We have this treasure from God, but we are like clay jars that hold the treasure. This shows that the great power is from God, not from us. We have troubles all around us, but we are not defeated. We do not know what to do, but we do not give up the hope of living. We are persecuted, but God does not leave us. We are hurt sometimes, but we are not destroyed. We carry the death of Jesus in our own bodies so that the life of Jesus can also be seen in our bodies. —2 CORINTHIANS 4:7–10 NCV

I find a sweet irony in the fact that I am part of a team called Women of Faith. I would love to think I have great faith in God, but I'm not sure that would be an adequate description of me. I vacillate between moments of great faith and groaning doubt. My misgivings are not about God or his ability to do great things, but rather about my part in the process. Sometimes on a Friday night as I sit in an arena filled with twenty thousand women, I find myself thinking, *Lord, I can't do this!* I feel like the little boy who brought his lunch to Jesus and then saw the size of the crowd and whispered to himself, *"Under catered!"*

Thankfully, over and over, the Lord has reminded me that the miracle wasn't in the boy's meager lunch but in the hands of the One who received it, blessed it, broke it, and fed more than five thousand people. Each weekend has its highlights, but nothing could have prepared any of us for what God was about to do on October 22, 2004. The events of the weekend would change us all for life.

MIRACLE IN MINNEAPOLIS

It started out much like every conference. We opened with a time of worship, which is just what everyone needs on a Friday night. It takes very careful planning, help, faith, husbands, babysitters, and divine intervention for twenty thousand women to find their way into their seats on a Friday night. I love to look out at the crowd and watch as exhausted expressions are lifted by the sound of twenty thousand women praising God together. It really is a remarkable experience to be part of such a choir.

Each member of the speaker team and our musical guests make time to be available on the concourse at breaks or at the end of each day so that women can have their books or CDs signed or simply talk with us for a few moments. Since I was the speaker that Friday night, I stayed after the evening event was over.

When I had finished signing books, I went down to the loading dock to catch the shuttle back to the hotel. I could tell immediately something was wrong. Usually the crew is either milling around joking with each other or in a meeting with Mary Graham, our president, reviewing the evening and preparing for the next day. Instead, on that evening they were standing around huddled in groups of two or three and no one was talking. I asked Mary what was wrong, and she told me that Pete Malvizzi, our lighting director, had suffered a massive brain aneurism and was in intensive care at a nearby hospital.

It was very hard to take in. One moment Pete was at the lighting board in control of a massive bank of stage lights—and the next, he had collapsed. The doctor gave no hope. He told our staff to get Pete's wife there immediately, that Pete was probably brain dead but was being kept alive on life support until his family could say good-bye.

The hospital was just two blocks away. So, as the next day wore on, all the speakers and Mary Graham went to the hospital two by two during the breaks. Marilyn Meberg and I went over to say good-bye to Pete during the morning break on Saturday.

I would love to tell you that when I saw Pete I had faith for a miracle, but his situation seemed hopeless. He was unconscious, hooked up to all sorts of machines, and he had a tube coming out of his skull draining blood from his brain. He looked so fragile as he lay there. Marilyn and I wept and shared our grief. And then we prayed a very simple prayer.

Dear Father,

Here is your servant Pete. In the room next door, Teresa, his wife, and his mom are sitting with broken hearts. At home Joey, his little boy, is waiting for his daddy to come home. God, would you please heal him? We love him, and we love you. Amen.

Marilyn and I returned to the conference. At the end of the day, Mary asked me to invite our audience to pray with us for Pete and his family. Before I prayed, I suggested that anyone who had a loved one in a life-threatening situation stand on behalf of that person while I prayed. Of course, we all stood for Pete and hundreds of women stood everywhere. It was unbelievable.

After the conference, Marilyn and Mary went back to the hospital. An hour or so later the crew arrived, having finished their day's work. Off and on the staff drifted in and out to express concern and condolence.

Pete seemed different. He was beginning to respond in a way he had not in twenty-four hours. Amazingly, his medical chart showed a change beginning at almost the precise moment we prayed in the arena.

Later, two neurosurgeons and a neurologist would say they considered Pete dead when he was brought into the hospital: "We would not have given a cent that he would survive." But by Sunday night, October 24, Pete was responding to very specific commands like, "Squeeze your right hand" and "Lift your left leg." The doctor said to our intercessor, Lana Bateman, "You guys must have some kind of prayer going!"

Pete is now back in his seat as our lighting director. He is a living miracle. But even as I thank God for that I am aware that on that same day other believers were crying out to God, on behalf of their loved ones, and that for reasons known only to God their lives were not spared. It is only human to want to know why? Why did God heal Pete and not others? Other men with wives and children who needed them just as much as Teresa and Joey need Pete died that day. There were believers calling out to God for a miracle and they didn't get one.

Why?

We can broaden the questions out beyond healing too.

> Why does God gives more gifts to some believers than others?

> Why do some Christians have much easier lives than others? Why does God says yes to some people's prayers and no to others?

I think all these concepts flow together with prayer. The gifts and the path we are given to walk on all spring out of our relationship with our Father. Since prayer is the most intimate form of communication between ourselves and God, if we believe God is favoring someone else over us, it will chip away at our trust and therefore our prayer life. We don't want to feel like our prayers are worthless, so we need to have a better understanding—and acceptance—of what God gives us and what he expects of us in return.

WHAT DID SHE GET?

When I was a little girl, one of my favorite nights of the year was the Sunday school Christmas party. We would all dress up in our finest Christmas attire and play games in the lower church hall until the big moment. Miss Burley would say, "Do you hear something?

I think I hear something." Everyone would settle down until you could hear a pin drop, and there it would be—the sound of sleigh bells.

By this point I would be beside myself with anticipation, waiting for the familiar "Ho! Ho! Ho!"

Then Father Christmas would come in carrying a sack over his shoulder. His cheeks would be rosy red from the cold night air, and we would all sing to him:

Jingle bells, jingle bells, jingle all the way
Oh what fun it is to ride on a one-horse open sleigh!

(The song never quite worked for me. I found it a bit embarrassing and was relieved Father Christmas appeared not to notice—or at least not to take offense. Well, I mean, everyone knows he uses reindeer, not a horse!)

After our song, we would sit in a circle and then Father Christmas would begin pulling gifts out of his big sack and calling out children's names. The gifts would be wrapped in brightly colored Christmas paper. When it was my turn, I could hardly walk I was so excited.

I remember one particular party when things didn't turn out quite as one girl hoped. I must have been eight or nine years old. I carried my gift back to my place in the circle as carefully as if I were carrying the baby Jesus himself. The girl beside me had already opened her gift. It was a Cindy doll—the Scottish equivalent of Barbie. (Not so skinny and less makeup!) She was thrilled with her gift . . . until I opened mine. I had received a mirror and brush and comb set. It was pink with small sparkles I thought were real diamonds.

When she saw my gift, the other girl said, "I would rather have that. Do you want to swap gifts?"

I said I would rather keep my gift, as Father Christmas chose it for me. I pointed out that her present was lovely too.

Then things got ugly. She had a total meltdown. Her final statement was that it was now clear to her Christmas was a joke! Father Christmas had favorites, and it was just not fair!

WHO DO YOU THINK YOU ARE?

Have you ever felt that way? Ever found yourself thinking, *God loves her more than he loves me. He's given her more than me, and he answers her prayers more often than he does mine.* If you have, I think there's some validity to what you might be feeling (I'll explain what I mean below). But how you respond to and interpret that reality makes all the difference.

I want to remind you of a story in Matthew's gospel:

[God's kingdom is] like a man going off on an extended trip. He called his servants together and delegated responsibilities. To one he gave five thousand dollars, to another two thousand, to a third one thousand, depending on their abilities. Then he left. Right off, the first servant went to work and doubled his master's investment. The second did the same. But the man with the single thousand dug a hole and carefully buried his master's money.

After a long absence, the master of those three servants came back and settled up with them. The one given five thousand dollars showed him how he had doubled his investment. His master commended him: "Good work! You did your job well. From now on be my partner."

The servant with the two thousand showed how he also had doubled his master's investment. His master commended him: "Good work! You did your job well. From now on be my partner."

The servant given one thousand said, "Master, I know you have high standards and hate careless ways, that you demand the best and make no allowances for error. I was afraid I might disappoint you, so I found a good hiding place and secured your money. Here it is, safe and sound down to the last cent."

The master was furious. "That's a terrible way to live! It's criminal to live cautiously like that! If you knew I was after the best, why did you do less than the least? The least you could have done would have been to invest the sum with the bankers, where at least I would have gotten a little interest. Take the thousand and give it to the one who risked the most. And get rid of this 'play-it-safe' who won't go out on a limb. Throw him out into utter darkness." (Matthew 25:14–30 MSG)

Several things are immediately clear from Christ's parable. The master does give more to some than he does to others. All that matters to him, however, is what each servant does with his or her gift. Just as the master doesn't expect the servant with a thousand dollars to produce the same as the one given five thousand, God doesn't expect the same from each of us. He just expects us to be good stewards with his gifts.

If we put that within the paradigm of the local church, one woman may be gifted as a speaker and leader and another may have a gift for flower arranging. What matters to God is that the one gifted in speaking and leadership brings everything she has to the table all the time. She can't look at the one doing the flower arranging and think, *She gets off with a light load whereas I have tons of preparation to do.* Nor should she think she needs to hold back because she doesn't want the other woman to think she's vain about her gift. What the other woman does should be irrelevant to her own gift and job.

Similarly, the woman with the gift in flower arranging is called to do everything within her abilities each time she arranges flowers as an offering to God. If she undervalues her gift because it is not as obvious a ministry as speaking and leading, she has missed the whole point—that God himself gave her that gift with specific tasks in mind. Focusing on anything less grieves God's heart.

I struggled with my own gift self-consciously for a while. During my first year with Women of Faith, I heard comments like these from women each weekend:

- "When you first got up on stage, I thought I wasn't going to like you."

- "I could relate to you more if you were fatter."

- "You looked so 'perfect,' I didn't think I could possibly have anything in common with you."

I began to feel that the minute my feet hit the stage, I had to do and say things to break down any barrier. Now, most days at home you will find me in jeans and a ball cap, but on conference weekends I spend time looking nice for the viewing audience. Many of the women barely make it to their seats for the start of the evening, having spent the day trying to make sure the household will function without them. They rush in and flop down . . . and then I prance up on stage in my suit and makeup.

So I would talk about coloring my hair and it turning green or struggling with my weight or my skin as a teenager or wearing high heels because I'm shrinking. For a time it was almost as if I felt I had to apologize for the fact that God chose me to be part of the Women of Faith team.

Until I read a passage in Paul's second letter to the church in Corinth:

> Remember, our Message is not about ourselves; we're proclaiming Jesus Christ, the Master. All we are is messengers, errand runners from Jesus for you. It started when God said, "Light up the darkness!" and our lives filled up with light as we saw and understood God in the face of Christ, all bright and beautiful. If you only look at us, you might well miss the brightness. We carry this precious Message around in the unadorned clay pots of our ordinary lives. That's to prevent anyone from confusing God's incomparable power with us. (2 Corinthians 4:5–7 MSG)

Paul saying to the church in Corinth, "We are just clay pots," is like saying to a church today, "We are just the cardboard boxes." Corinth was a busy shipping port and a wealthy city. The most common receptacle to contain dry goods or transport items from one city to another was a clay pot. They came in all sizes imaginable— the FedEx boxes of the day. So what Paul was saying in essence was (and I paraphrase):

We're just the containers, the cardboard boxes. We are not the point. It is up to God what he puts in each box. A box never turns to the shipper and asks why he only got two glasses while another box got six. What is in the box says nothing about the box and everything about the shipper. All the box is expected to do is to contain what it has been given, to guard and protect the contents.

I found this so liberating! If God decided to put six things in my box and ten things in Billy Graham's box and four in Aunt Hilda's box, that was God's deal, not mine. I couldn't imagine a box apologizing for what it had been asked to carry or wanting to carry more or something different. The box was not the point; it was just the receptacle.

I wonder how many of us resent others' gifts or the size of our box compared to theirs. Or we hold back because we're embarrassed about our own gifts. If we are, it's pointless—a waste of time and energy. If God puts ten things in your box and three in mine, does that mean he loves you more? Absolutely not! God is as crazy about me as he is about you. With that knowledge in hand, nothing else should matter.

That's why the comment from Gore Vidal I included at the beginning of this chapter saddens me. To think that every time a friend of his succeeds he feels as if part of him dies seems a lonely and confining way to live. From that place you are not free. You are not liberated to celebrate the successes of others or even to accept their joy when you succeed.

For the first ten years I was in America, I was a Christian recording artist. My whole life was recording and touring. Each year at the Dove Awards (the gospel music awards), I was a bit of a well-intentioned joke with my friends. The word was that if you wanted to win an award, make sure you're in the same category as Sheila because she never wins. I never did, and I never have. I have watched Sandi Patty win more Doves than one would expect to see in an aviary, but not one flew the coop and headed my way!

The truth is, though, I adore Sandi and I love her voice. The fact that God put a lot more high notes and glorious texture in her box than he did in mine is his business. I get to celebrate Sandi. And the sweet thing is she celebrates me too. (On a side note, at one of our Women of Faith conferences, Sandi asked me if she could give me a vocal suggestion for something "fancy" I could try with the ending of my song. I tried it . . . and let's just say I didn't quite pull it off. I could hardly finish the song for laughing! We decided it's better for me just to stick with what's in my box!)

We are the vessels, and the whole point is for Christ to be seen in us. Can you imagine what an impact it would have on the world if everyone who follows Christ lived like this? If we all woke up every morning and thanked God for the gifts we have been given and asked for opportunities that day to use them for his glory? He is the one who is watching. He is the one who gave us our gifts, and to question that is to insinuate God got it wrong.

I'm not saying this is always easy. In fact, I'll admit sometimes it's hard to live on planet earth and remember we are called to live for an audience of one! The trouble is that some gifts receive immediate praise and recognition, and others don't. We must keep in mind whom we're working for. If we're dependent on the approval of others, life will be very discouraging. But if we wait only on the Lord, his love will uplift us no matter what. To God, there are no small jobs or menial tasks. He misses nothing. He sees all the late-night laundry and lunches packed. He sees the extra work your boss never credits you for. He sees it all. If we can grasp this, it will help with all the petty (or not-so-petty) indignities in life.

As far as I am concerned, I work for God. He is my boss, and he is my King. So whether I am writing this book, recording a CD, speaking to twenty thousand women, or sitting in the carpool lane waiting for Christian, it doesn't matter. No one thing that I am called to do is more important than another; all that matters is my heart.

BUT WHAT ABOUT PRAYER?

Yes, what about God seeming to choose "favorites" when it comes to prayer? We've talked about God allotting what could be considered greater gifts to one person versus another. Is it then true that God favors one over another in prayer? It can certainly seem that way sometimes.

Barry, Christian, and I were driving one Monday night to the first soccer game of the 2007 season. As we got closer to the field, I asked Christian if he had any special prayer requests. He said, "Yes, let's pray that we win!"

I laughed and asked him, "Christian, what do you think God will do if there is a boy on the other team praying exactly the same prayer?"

He replied with a smile, "Quick, let's get our prayer in first!"

When we think of a father figure being asked for the same thing by two different children, we are tied to our human understanding of love. God's thoughts are far higher than ours (Isaiah 55:9), and his plans are always for our good—to prosper and not to harm us (Jeremiah 29:11). The trouble is how we interpret the word *prosper*.

When I was pregnant with Christian, I had a very honest conversation with a friend of mine. We are the same age, and she longs to be married and be a mom. I married Barry when I was thirty-eight and was gifted with a child at forty. She told me that it was hard thinking that we both came before God about the same time with the same requests, and God gave me a husband and a child while she had received neither. I ached for my friend. Her questions make total sense to me. It would seem as if God has *prospered* me more than my friend.

But if we're to take the whole "clay pot" lesson to heart, we have to resist believing this is true. If the whole point of our lives is to become more like Christ and be a conduit for the love of God, then we will each be given different paths to take—which may or may not correlate to our prayers. Some paths seem more attractive than others, but no one really knows the burdens another carries. What I am convinced of is that God loves his children. I don't know why he answers one woman's prayer one way and another woman's prayer differently, only that he has a reason for it.

One of the ways we can measure whether we are at peace in the love of God is by asking ourselves whether we fall into Gore Vidal's camp—unable to celebrate Christ shining through another's life—or whether we are able to recognize God's wisdom as he lovingly hand-packs each cardboard box himself. Because only when we can do that—when we can accept his hand working differently in your life as opposed to mine, answering each prayer in his own time and understanding—can we truly be at peace with God. As I said earlier, believing that God is not listening to us dampens our relationship with him. But taking joy in living out his plan for us—that's freeing!

God loves us. That's all we need to focus on.

> *O, let the light stream in,*
> *The glorious light of day,*
> *That o'er the face of nature sheds*
> *A bright and genial ray;*
> *We need its beams our steps to guide,*
> *Ere daily toils begin,*
> *Then open wide the door of prayer,*
> *And let the light stream in.*
> *Let the light stream in,*
> *Let the light stream in,*
> *Then open wide the door of prayer,*
> *And let the light stream in.*
>
> *O, let the light stream in,*
> *The light of Gospel day,*
> *That shineth through the righteousness*
> *Of Christ, the Truth, the Way;*
> *'Twill teach us how by faith in Him*
> *Immortal souls to win,*
> *Then open wide our willing hearts,*
> *And let the light stream in.*
> *Let the light stream in,*
> *Let the light stream in,*
> *Then open wide our willing hearts,*
> *And let the light stream in.*

O, let the light stream in
Where homes are dark and drear,
The light of God's eternal love,
That conquers every fear;
Its gentle smile new joys may wake,
Where sorrow long hath been,
Then open wide the door of hope,
And let the light shine in.
Let the light stream in,
Let the light stream in,
Then open wide the door of hope,
And let the light stream in.

—FANNY CROSBY

part 3

the
plan

9

How Do I Know I Heard God's Voice?

Was It Him or Last Night's Pizza?

"I have some great news for you," he told me.

"What's that?" I enquired.

"God told me that I'm going to marry you."

"Well," I replied, "as soon as he tells me too I'll get right back to you."

—A CONVERSATION AT THE LONDON SCHOOL OF THEOLOGY, SUMMER 1977

The LORD called Samuel a third time, and Samuel got up and went to Eli and said, "Here I am; you called me." Then Eli realized that the LORD was calling the boy. So Eli told Samuel, "Go and lie down, and if he calls you, say, 'Speak, LORD, for your servant is listening.'" So Samuel went and lay down in his place. The LORD came and stood there, calling as at the other times, "Samuel! Samuel!" Then Samuel said, "Speak, for your servant is listening." —1 SAMUEL 3:8–10

I read a sign in a storefront recently that said, "We sell everything you need to tell the one you love you'd marry her all over again."

Think about that statement for a moment. The implication is clear: gifts communicate love. One might reasonably assume the more you spend, the more heartfelt the sentiment. But in reality that's not the case. Commercialism is a subtle invader—it creeps up on us and can sound very convincing, but it is a poor substitute for communication and relationship.

I am a big fan of NBC's sitcom *The Office*. One particular episode illustrates my point about gifts. It's Christmas, and the staff of this Scranton-based paper company decides to play Secret Santa. They each pull a name from a hat and promise to buy that person a gift for about twenty dollars. The boss, Michael Scott (played brilliantly by Steve Carell), splurges on his gift and buys an iPod that costs about four hundred dollars. When it's time to open the gifts, Ryan, who receives the iPod, is overwhelmed and embarrassed. But when Michael opens his gift from his Secret Santa, it is a hand-knitted oven mitt. Hating it, he pitches a fit and ruins the whole day.

Michael tries to justify his outburst by saying the gift he received meant, "I only value you an oven-mitt's worth," whereas his gift said, "I value you an iPod's worth!"

Michael, of course, missed the point of the gift giving. He's not alone—it's getting easier and easier to do in our world as commercialism takes the place of heartfelt gratitude.

Let me unpack that idea a little before you try to knock me off my soapbox. Take Mother's Day, for example. What is it about? To my understanding it's about pausing for a moment and reflecting on God's goodness in giving us a mother to love and parent us with grace and wisdom, and then expressing that thankfulness back to her. Instead we've turned it into one more spend-fest. We're attacked from all angles—television, stores, radio—about the need to express our love in material form. It's hard to get away. We're told flowers are a must to demonstrate our caring. We're told a sentimental card is required. We're told diamonds are the only way to say, "I love you."

Well, no, they are not. Diamonds don't say, "I love you." *People* say, "I love you."

Obviously there are times when we give gifts to symbolize our affection, but that should never take the place of expressing our hearts to each other. When Barry and I were first married, for my birthday or Christmas or Valentine's Day he would give me very expensive, handmade cards that were covered in jewels or lace. They were beautiful and I appreciated them, but eventually I told him what I would love even more would be a simple card that told me how he felt about me.

What I'm trying to say is that we are losing the art of listening to each other and expressing with our own words the content of our hearts. We live in a very fast-paced society where money can easily take the place of time. This carries over into our prayer life. If we're so caught up in the material world that we can't relate to people here on earth on a personal level and share our inner self, how are we going to relate to God? As far as I know, they don't make flower deliveries to heaven!

The really sad fact about all of this is that in many cases, our obsession with material love not only hinders our true relationships with others but actually harms them. In the spring of 2007, ABC News carried the story of what happened to Jack Whittaker, the recipient of $315 million—the largest lotto win ever. His only desire was to spoil his granddaughter, so he gave her $2,000 each week and bought her four cars. She was seventeen years old.

Yet ABC News reported in their *20/20* story on April 6, 2007, that Mr. Whittaker wished he had torn the ticket up—that he had never won the lottery. Why? Because his beloved granddaughter used his monetary gifts to become addicted to drugs. After several years in a downward spiral, she was found dead, her body wrapped in a tarp and thrown behind an old car.

What had Jack been trying to do for his granddaughter? Nothing more than tell her he loved her—in the way our pop culture dictates, by giving her stuff. But "stuff" can kill. In her case, it did.

NO SUBSTITUTE FOR PRAYER

Just as money can't buy me love, nothing should *ever* take the place of my own personal time with God, where I as his follower listen for his voice.

I love to read good Christian books. I enjoy attending events where I have the opportunity to hear speakers relate their experiences with God or teach on a particular passage of Scripture. I mean, if you think about it, it's what I do. I'd better enjoy it! But it's not enough to know what someone else is learning from God, encouraging though that may be. I need to be learning and growing too.

So many times we forget that. We hear people telling us that the way to God is clearer through something or someone else. That if we just read this book, the author will tell us how to reach God. That if we send money to that ministry, someone will talk to God and receive an answer on our behalf.

Rubbish! God talks to his people through his Word, through the counsel of godly friends, and to our own hearts through the Holy Spirit.

In my twenties and thirties, I was surrounded by people who seemed to hear from God on a remarkably frequent level. Almost every week, people reported that God was showing up and giving them specific directions. But those kinds of experiences never happened to me. I worried that somehow I was missing God—that everyone else had a better listening ear than I did. Perhaps I was destined to hear from God secondhand.

What about you? What do you rely on when you want to hear from God on a specific issue or a general direction? Do you sit and wait, hoping you'll find direction in a book or through someone else? Or do you take time to pray? And not just pray, but to listen to and to meditate on God's Word?

Yes, that's right. I'm saying that prayer is sometimes just the beginning of the conversation. Sometimes we need more. And unfortunately, we don't always know exactly how to go about it. So many of the spiritual disciplines that used to be practiced by believers have, to a large extent, been lost. Meditation, solitude, and fasting are elements that are often missing from our lives. It takes an intentional choice to carve out time in our overfull schedules to listen to the voice of God. Perhaps we have lived such busy lives for so long that we have forgotten how, or perhaps we have never learned to listen for God in that way. But Jesus assured us that when we look past all the books and speakers and seek to commune with him, we will know his voice:

I am the Good Shepherd. I know my own sheep and my own sheep know me. In the same way, the Father knows me and I know the Father. I put the sheep before myself, sacrificing myself if necessary. You need to know that I have other sheep in addition to those in this pen. I need to gather and bring them, too. They'll also recognize my voice. Then it will be one flock, one Shepherd. (John 10:14–16 MSG)

I am not suggesting that we reject godly counsel from those we trust and respect. One of the ways God speaks to us is through the wise counsel of other believers. But he loves one-on-one conversation. I'd like us to look at the lives of two people whom I hope will help us gain a greater understanding of how to listen for the voice of God. One thought she would never be able to celebrate a Mother's Day and one didn't recognize the voice of God when he heard it.

HANNAH — PRAYING WITH PERSISTENCE

I love the story of Hannah. She had a wonderful husband, Elkanah, who adored her. But there was another woman in the picture— Penninah, Elkanah's other wife. Penninah had given Elkanah children, but Hannah had not and it broke her heart. Once a year the family would make the trip to the tabernacle at Shiloh to worship God and offer sacrifices for his goodness to them. Children were recognized as a blessing from God, and each year Penninah made the trip a nightmare for Hannah, mocking her lack of children.

Elkanah was distraught to see Hannah so upset. He loved her very much and asked her if his love for her was not enough. Hannah loved her husband, but she desperately wanted a child.

During one trip to the temple, Hannah slipped off by herself to pray. She was so distraught and grief stricken as she prayed that the priest, Eli, thought she had been drinking. She told him that she was not that kind of woman but, rather, she had been in true anguish of soul, asking God for a child.

In those days, before the birth of Christ, the priest was the direct link to God. When Eli told her to go in peace and God wouldgrant her request, Hannah received the answer from Eli as if it had come from God.

There are times when we have prayed and prayed about something for a long time and then, just as Hannah heard from the priest and knew the answer was from God, we, too, receive an inner assurance that God has heard our prayer and it's time to stop weeping and start thanking him for his answer. The Bible tells us,

> Don't fret or worry. Instead of worrying, pray. Let petitions and praises shape your worries into prayers, letting God know your concerns. Before you know it, a sense of God's wholeness, everything coming together for good, will come and settle you down. It's wonderful what happens when Christ displaces worry at the center of your life. (Philippians 4:6–7 MSG)

Hannah longed to hear from God. Once she had the assurance that God had heard her request and would answer her prayer, everything changed. She had something to eat and her whole countenance was lifted. Almost immediately upon returning home, Hannah became pregnant. She named her son Samuel, which means "Name of God," because God had given him to her.

On the next family trip to the temple, Hannah did not go. She asked Elkanah if she could take Samuel and give him back to God's service in the temple when he was weaned (usually at four years of age). Elkanah honored her request.

We don't know what happened in those four years, but when we see the young man Samuel became, it's clear he learned a lot about God from his faithful mother. Honoring her promise to God,

Hannah took young Samuel back to the temple, where he was trained by Eli for God's service. I can't imagine what that must have been like to take her three- or four-year-old child and leave him, but Hannah obviously had a strong relationship with God and total confidence that she was doing the right thing and that God would watch over Samuel. She prayed one of the most beautiful prayers ever recorded in Scripture as she worshipped her Lord before returning home.

> I'm walking on air. I'm laughing at my rivals. I'm dancing my salvation. Nothing and no one is holy like GOD, no rock mountain like our God. Don't dare talk pretentiously—not a word of boasting, ever!
>
> For GOD knows what's going on. He takes the measure of everything that happens. The weapons of the strong are smashed to pieces, while the weak are infused with fresh strength. The well-fed are out begging in the streets for crusts, while the hungry are getting second helpings. The barren woman has a houseful of children, while the mother of many is bereft.
>
> GOD brings death and GOD brings life, brings down to the grave and raises up. GOD brings poverty and GOD brings wealth; he lowers, he also lifts up. He puts poor people on their feet again; he rekindles burned-out lives with fresh hope, restoring dignity and respect to their lives—a place in the sun! (1 Samuel 2:1–9 MSG)

From Hannah's life we can learn several lessons. She was patient and persistent in her prayer life. She kept coming before God with her request, and even in her moments of despair, she shared her grief with God. Hannah never stopped asking and never stopped listening. When God answered her prayer favorably, she recognized where the answer came from and gave back to him. (In a nice postscript to Hannah's life, after she gave Samuel to the Lord, she gave birth to three more boys and two girls!)

When you are longing to hear from God, take time away from the noise of life and practice the discipline of waiting quietly in his presence. Just as you long to hear from him, you have a Father who longs to speak to his children.

SAMUEL—HEARING GOD'S VOICE

Samuel became a junior priest. Each year Hannah would return to the temple with a new linen robe for him. We don't know much about Samuel's early work, just that he grew in stature and in favor with God and men. That's quite a commendation to be favored by God and respected by men as well. Such an honor was rare in those days when Israel was in trouble spiritually and politically. Samuel had been chosen by God to have an impact on Israel's history at a very difficult time. Eli was a well-meaning priest, but his sons were out of control and abused their role as priests to get what they wanted from the people they were supposed to be serving.

Samuel loved Eli but as yet had no personal relationship with God. One night, several hours before dawn, young Samuel heard someone call his name. As he and Eli slept in the temple, he assumed that it was the old man who was calling for him. The priest told him that he hadn't called out and told the boy to go back to sleep. It happened a second time and then a third. Then Eli realized that God was calling Samuel. I think it took three times for Eli to realize what was happening because we read that this took place at "a time when the revelation of GOD was rarely heard or seen" (1 Samuel 3:1 MSG).

Eli told Samuel that if he heard the voice again, he should reply, "Speak, God. I'm your servant, ready to listen." So Samuel went back to bed. When he heard the voice call his name again, he replied, "Speak. I am your servant, ready to listen." He didn't address him as God because he didn't know him as God—yet. But Samuel went on to become one of the most powerful prophets in all of Israel's history. It became widely recognized that God was talking again through the young priest, Samuel.

In many ways we live in times like Samuel. You only have to watch the news or read a newspaper to be aware the evil that is rampant in our world. We hear stories of those who are called to be servants to God's people just as Eli's sons were and then they are arrested for misappropriating funds or embezzlement. Perhaps you are discouraged by the times you live in and wonder how you can hear God's voice in the midst of all the evil in this world. Take heart from Samuel's life. God looks for those who still have hearts open to him and gives them ears to hear his voice.

Do you recognize moments like that from your own life? Perhaps you have felt a prompting to do something or go somewhere or stop somewhere for coffee where you wouldn't normally, and only in retrospect can you see the hand of God. There might have been someone there who just needed a word of encouragement or you might have seen a book that answers something you've been asking God about.

We have a Father who loves to talk with his children, so listen for his still, small voice.

DIFFERENT DAYS

We don't live in the days of Samuel or Moses—the days when God spoke only through prophets or kings. We live in a time when God speaks to each of his children through his Word and through the Holy Spirit and through wise counsel. Whenever I have found myself in a place of wanting to hear God's voice before I move in one direction or another, I ask myself several questions:

- *Does anything in this situation go against the revealed Word of God?* A young woman told me she believed she was supposed to leave her husband because she had fallen in love with someone else. But when an emotional response such as that is held up against the plumb line of God's Word, it doesn't measure up.

- *Do I feel a great urgency and stress to do something right away?* When I feel a compulsion to move quickly, I wait. God is a God of order and peace.

- *Do those whom I respect and trust sense God's presence in this situation too?* There will be times when God will ask us to step outside of what others understand, but it has been my experience that those situations are rare. When God does that, I believe there will be the gift of unusual peace and grace.

If we can follow these three guidelines, our lives will be much simpler and more fulfilled.

God is a God of peace, and when you feel all churned up about a decision or separated from others because you feel compelled to make a move that those you love and trust question, it is usually wise to wait. Hannah had to wait a long time for a child, but she never gave up hope. It took time for Samuel to learn God's voice, but once he had, he never forgot and others around him recognized that God spoke to Samuel. God loves to talk to his children, so ask for ears to hear and a heart to know his voice.

Master, speak! Thy servant heareth,
Waiting for Thy gracious word,
Longing for Thy voice that cheereth;
Master! let it now be heard.
I am listening, Lord, for Thee:
What hast Thou to say to me?

Speak to me by name, O Master,
Let me know it is to me;
Speak, that I may follow faster,
With a step more firm and free,
Where the Shepherd leads the flock,
In the shadow of the rock.

Master, speak! and make me ready,
When Thy voice is truly heard,
With obedience glad and steady
Still to follow every word.
I am listening, Lord, for Thee:
Master, speak! O, speak to me!
—FRANCES R. HAVERGAL

10

Can I Ask God for Anything if I Have Enough Faith?

Dear God, Will You Make Me Taller?

Is the Son of God praying in me, or am I dictating to Him? . . . Prayer is not simply getting things from God, that is a most initial form of prayer; prayer is getting into perfect communion with God. If the Son of God is formed in us by regeneration, He will press forward in front of our common sense and change our attitude to the things about which we pray. —Oswald Chambers

I tell you the truth, anyone who believes in me will do the same works I have done, and even greater works, because I am going to be with the Father. You can ask for anything in my name, and I will do it, so that the Son can bring glory to the Father. Yes, ask me for anything in my name, and I will do it! —John 14:12–14 NLT

When I was sixteen, it became apparent to me that I was stuck at five feet four inches in height. I wanted to be taller, though, so I decided to make it a matter of prayer. It made perfect sense to me to ask God to fix my height deficit—after all, God made me, so God could stretch me out a bit.

I prayed a very fervent prayer for a few nights, to no avail. I knew I must be doing something wrong—the block in the prayer pipeline had to be on my end. And the more I thought about it, the clearer it became: I was being selfish, asking for something without giving something in return. So I attempted to make a sort of "deal" with God. I told him that if I awoke the next morning and was two inches taller, then I would be a missionary. It stood to reason that one would be grateful for the extra height on the mission field, I reasoned, as one cannot, presumably, wear heels. When I went to sleep that night, I was absolutely sure I would wake up taller and be obliged to start packing.

I don't know whether God wanted to spare Africa or spare me, but my height remained stuck at five feet four inches. I was genuinely disappointed and concluded it was my lack of faith. It was clear to me from Scripture that if you ask God for anything and your faith doesn't waver, then he'll answer. It sounded like such a watertight formula:

> But let him ask in faith, with no doubting, for he who doubts is like a wave of the sea driven and tossed by the wind. For let not that man suppose that he will receive anything from the Lord; he is a double-minded man, unstable in all his ways. (James 1:6–8 NKJV)

That scripture served to confirm in my mind that I must have wavered in my faith and so God was waiting until I was resolute and unswerving.

I was left with a dilemma: if God's Word says that we can ask for anything in his name, then obviously the onus is on us to pray with unshakable faith. But where do we get that kind of faith? I was convinced that if God answered just one of my very specific prayers, then my faith would grow (therefore allowing me to ask for even bigger things).

Cause and effect, you see.

Yet because God didn't answer my prayers, I was never given that chance to prove my faith. Which conceivably made my faith waver even more (therefore making me have even fewer answers to prayer than I might have before).

That old cause and effect thing again.

It was an interesting conundrum. And as the years passed, it became clear this was a question many believers have wrestled with and come to varying conclusions about.

STANDING ON THE PROMISES

When I was in my early twenties, I had the privilege of working with British pop superstar Cliff Richard. Although he has never made a huge breakthrough in America, he is a major celebrity in the rest of the world. He holds the record of being the only artist to make the United Kingdom singles charts in all of its active decades, 1950 to the present. And he is the first British pop star to be knighted by Queen Elizabeth, before Sir Paul McCartney and Sir Elton John.

He is also a very committed follower of Jesus Christ. Once a year, Cliff has a tour to raise money for the Christian charity Tear Fund, and for several years I was Cliff's opening act for the tour. This may sound as if I was chosen from a large group of Christian artists such as we have in the United States, but that was not the case. There were about four of us and the other three were busy! But it was a huge honor for me (and incidentally the only time I have ever ridden in a Rolls-Royce—wow!).

I got to know many of Cliff's loyal fans fairly well, but there is one whose story has stayed with me. She was a very sweet, single lady with a shy demeanor. She wore no makeup and dressed as if she were attending a very conservative church, not a pop concert. But each evening many of the fans would stand at the stage door for a long time hoping to get Cliff's autograph, and she was often in the crowd, following the show from town to town.

I asked her one night why she attended so many of the concerts, and she told me she was going to marry Cliff. She must have seen my surprised expression, because she told me she knew that seemed like quite a leap, but she was a believer and she had asked in Jesus' name, with no doubts at all.

I knew it was *possible* that Cliff might marry her, but very unlikely; I had seen Cliff sign a CD or photo for her, and although he was kind, as he was to all his fans, it didn't go beyond that. It seemed to me that she had substituted wishful thinking for faith.

In situations like this, it is easy to slip into a spoiled-child mentality, as if God "owes" us and all we have to do is want something enough and it will happen. Matthew 6:33 notes we are called to grow up and mature in our faith and prayer life and to seek first God's kingdom and righteousness, but it's easy to skip over the first part of the verse ("But seek first the kingdom of God and His righteousness") right to, "And all these things shall be added to you" (NKJV).

In my own life I know that the more I intentionally seek God's kingdom and his heart, the more my desires change. But this woman was not allowing God to work in and renew her life. As I thought of the years passing and her holding on to her belief regarding Cliff, my heart ached. I wondered how many nice Christian guys she'd met but never paid attention to because she thought she was standing on the promises of God. I wondered, too, if her faith continued strong or if she was beginning to waver, as each concert passed without recognition from Cliff.

And, more important, I wondered if that's what God wanted her to do.

My friend Dr. Henry Cloud once told me of a woman who called into his radio show one day saying she had so much faith God could bring the right man to her door that she didn't even need to go outside. Dr. Cloud told her that unless she wanted to marry the FedEx guy or a Jehovah's Witness, she might want to reconsider.

It's a sad but true fact. I have talked to many women who have virtually put their lives on hold waiting for God to show up with the answer they are standing in faith for. I think of a woman I heard about. Her husband walked out on her, leaving her to raise their children by herself. She believed absolutely that she should trust God and not the court system to help her. What faith meant to her was that when her husband asked her to sign all their assets over to him, she did. In her heart she believed that if she prayed hard enough and refused to look to anyone else for help apart from her heavenly Father, then he would honor her faithful prayers and her husband would come home.

Unfortunately he did not, and she was left in very dire straits. This woman was not an immature Christian but a woman who has loved and followed God for many years. She wanted nothing more than to show God that no matter how circumstances looked, she believed in his ability to move mountains.

I have seen this type of situation over and over again, whether a prayer for a loved one, a request for a spouse, the gift of a child, or even that God would clear the path into a public ministry. What went wrong in these situations? To me, these people seemed committed, and I trust their prayers were infinitely more important than my desire for two more inches. Why, then, did their prayers go unanswered?

THE MISSING KEY

I was walking through a department store in the mall one day when I heard someone call my name. I looked up but didn't recognize the woman who was beckoning me over to her makeup counter. For a moment I thought it might be one of those offers of a free makeover that end up costing you an arm and a leg and send you off looking like Barbie's cousin. But I was wrong. Instead, after explaining she'd read several of my books and heard me speak, she asked a question.

"How can I find the missing key? I've been praying and praying, but nothing's happening."

"I'm not sure I know what you mean," I said. "What missing key? What are you praying for exactly?"

"For the door. I'm looking for the key to the door. . . . I mean, I know that I'm supposed to be in ministry, but I don't know where the key is," she said.

"What makes you think there is a key?" I asked.

"There has to be," she said. "I have a heart to be in ministry and I've asked God to open the door and nothing has happened. So I must be missing something—some key, some prayer. I've tried every-thing I can think of and nothing is happening, so I'm just waiting."

I told her I believe that wherever we are in life we are ministers of the gospel. Whether you are bagging groceries or leading a Bible study, when you see all of life as sacred and an offering to God, that is ministry. But I could see that was not the answer she wanted. She wanted a specific answer that met her needs, and she wanted it now.

This is a common cry. Not just from us, but through the ages. It is heard over and over in the Bible:

⋅› "How long, O LORD? Will you forget me forever? How long will you hide your face from me?" (Psalm 13:1).

⋅› "Answer me quickly, O LORD; my spirit fails. Do not hide your face from me" (Psalm 143:7).

⋅› "Listen to my prayer, O God, do not ignore my plea; hear me and answer me. My thoughts trouble me and I am dis-traught" (Psalm 55:1–2).

⋅› "How long, O LORD, must I call for help, but you do not listen? Or cry out to you, 'Violence!' but you do not save?" (Habakkuk 1:1–2).

I celebrate the fact that God accepts us in all of our humanity. We are allowed to ask questions, to be sad when we don't get the answers we long for, to grieve over losses no matter how insignificant they may seem to others. Yet, as I think about the requests I myself have made to God through the years and the stories I have heard from others, I see one big problem: when we take what we want and try to twist God's arm to answer us, we shift from worshippers to spoiled children. We move from servant to master. My desire to be taller, the fan's desire to marry Cliff, or the department store employee's desire for a ministry all add up to the same thing: *Here is what I want, Father. I am asking in Jesus' name so you have to give it to me.*

That is not the heart Jesus displayed while he walked in human flesh. When Jesus prayed in the Garden of Gethsemane, the pattern he modeled in agony and tears was this:

- *Total honesty and vulnerability.* "Going a little ahead, he fell on his face, praying, 'My Father, if there is any way, get me out of this'" (Matthew 26:39 MSG).

- *Total surrender to God's plan.* "But please, not what I want. You, what do you want?" (Matthew 26:39 MSG).

Jesus lived every moment of his life with an awareness of what mattered. He knew that the purpose of this life we are gifted with is to bring honor and glory to God, not to make life easy or comfortable for us. His first cry illustrates how hard it is at times to embrace God's will, and yet his second cry reaches out and grasps hold of whatever would bring glory to his Father.

I want to live like that!

THE REAL KEY

As I read over Jesus' promise to his friends recorded at the beginning of this chapter, two short but vital phrases jumped out at me: "You can ask for anything *in my name*, and I will do it, so that the Son can *bring glory to the Father*" (John 14:13 NLT; emphasis added).

If you can, imagine for a moment that before Jesus left this earth he commissioned you to represent him (which he did!). So, when you come to the Father with your prayer requests you are representing the person of Jesus, coming in his authority. I believe that if we carried that awareness with us, it would impact how we pray and what we ask for. If I take that paradigm and apply it to my situation as a teenager, it would be hard to imagine praying, "Father God, I am here in Jesus' name on kingdom business. Thank you for sending Jesus to be executed in my place and to give me a new life. Now, I am here today to request that I be two inches taller by morning."

That hardly sounds like a credible prayer from a representative of Christ's mission on earth. How would being two inches taller bring any glory to God's name? That kind of prayer reflects an earthbound perspective of what matters. Also, it is a temporary measure. This earthly body we have is simply a container for the glory of God.

But what about the woman who wanted to marry the pop star? There would be nothing intrinsically wrong with praying for that, but the focus might shift if she lived with an acute awareness of being Christ's ambassador on earth. It might become, "Father, if the two of us being married would bring glory to you and extend your kingdom, then I welcome it and you know that I would love it if it were possible. If not, I welcome your will."

But what about my friend who believed God would restore her marriage? That's a far more complicated situation. It would seem to always be God's will to restore a family, but within every marriage there are two hearts and two wills. The gift of free will is an amazing one that God grants to every human heart. He could have preprogrammed us to love and obey him, but he didn't. He allows us to choose our path. And unfortunately, that—along with the temptations and trials of this world—opens us up to failure when we forget to make our will fall in line with God's will. Therefore, like my friend, we can petition God for something according to his will, but we can't make the other person in the situation respond in the same manner.

So we return to my original question: can we ask God for anything if our faith is strong enough? Well, yes. But is that really the right question? It's not so much about our level of faith as what we put our faith in. Are we asking for the right things? Are we seeking God's will in the situation? And are we comfortable with his response if things don't end up the way we wanted?

I hope so. It's not always easy. But as I said before, we have a guide. When you meditate on the life of Christ you see how often he pulled away from the crowd to be alone with his Father. He lived every moment of his time on earth as a representative of the heart of God. Looking at that and longing to be like Jesus are changing the way I pray—as I hope it will change yours. I believe we are encouraged to pour our hearts and desires out to God, but the cry of Christ's heart that I long to be daily the cry of mine is, "But please, not what I want. You—what do you want?"

Standing on the promises of Christ my King,
Through eternal ages let His praises ring,
Glory in the highest, I will shout and sing,
Standing on the promises of God.

can i ask God for anything if i have enough faith?

Standing, standing,
Standing on the promises of God my Savior;
Standing, standing,
I'm standing on the promises of God.

Standing on the promises that cannot fail,
When the howling storms of doubt and fear assail,
By the living Word of God I shall prevail,
Standing on the promises of God.

Standing on the promises I now can see
Perfect, present cleansing in the blood for me;
Standing in the liberty where Christ makes free,
Standing on the promises of God.

Standing on the promises of Christ the Lord,
Bound to Him eternally by love's strong cord,
Overcoming daily with the Spirit's sword,
Standing on the promises of God.

Standing on the promises I cannot fall,
Listening every moment to the Spirit's call
Resting in my Savior as my all in all,
Standing on the promises of God.
—R. Kelso Carter

11

Can I Question God?

Is Anybody Out There?

But, might some say, where was Tess's guardian angel? Perhaps, like that other god of whom the ironical Tishbite spoke, he was talking, or he was pursuing, or he was in a journey, or he was sleeping and not to be awakened. —FROM *TESS OF THE D'URBERVILLES* BY THOMAS HARDY

Then the disciples of John reported to him concerning all these things. And John, calling two of his disciples to him, sent them to Jesus, saying, "Are You the Coming One, or do we look for another?" When the men had come to Him, they said, "John the Baptist has sent us to You, saying, 'Are You the Coming One, or do we look for another?'" And that very hour He cured many of infirmities, afflictions, and evil spirits; and to many blind He gave sight. Jesus answered and said to them, "Go and tell John the things you have seen and heard: that the blind see, the lame walk, the lepers are cleansed, the deaf hear, the dead are raised, the poor have the gospel preached to them. And blessed is he who is not offended because of Me." —LUKE 7:18–23 NKJV

Do you ever find yourself asking why? Not just on the big life issues, but on the small stuff—the day-to-day things that can be quite simple but no less frustrating. I ask myself on a daily basis, for example, "Why can't I remember to take my vitamins?" (I mean, how hard is it to remember that?) Or "Why is it that when I'm twenty minutes into one diet program, a different one seems more appealing and effective" (even though that's the one I was on when this one sounded better)?

One morning I was staring at myself in the bathroom mirror, asking myself one of those questions: "Why do I look so pale?" I never noticed that my skin was pale when I lived in Tennessee, but since moving to Texas, the difference in my skin tone and that of the other mothers in car pool is quite striking. They look as if they have just gotten off a horse after an invigorating ride, and I look like I got off a sled after the Iditarod.

I must have asked the question out loud because a couple of days later, Barry handed me a card. On the front it read, "May all your dreams come true." Inside was a gift card for a place called Planet Tan.

I looked at the card for a moment before feeling compelled to say, "Barry, this was so sweet of you, but I'm not going in another tanning bed as long as I live. I tried it once, and it was like being laid to rest in a casket with very bright lights!"

"No, this is different," he insisted. "This is a spray-on tan!" He seemed inordinately excited.

"Barry, Barry, Barry," I replied. "If you think I'm getting into a bathing suit and allowing someone from Rent-a-Tan to hose me down, you are seriously mistaken!"

"No, it's not like that," he said. "You have your own private booth. I've paid for it, so do you think you could just try it once?"

"Okay . . . once," I relented. "But if I end up looking as if I was born in Bombay, you can explain that to my mother!"

Later that day I walked into the establishment and was greeted by several "golden" people. I lifted my hand in the Vulcan signal. "Greetings, Golden People. I come in peace."

One girl took me back to my room. The booth looked like a space capsule.

"Okay," she began. "Take all your clothes off and—"

"Whoa, hold it right there," I said. "All my clothes? I'm a Baptist!"

"You can have this," she said.

I looked at what she had in her hand. It was a tiny paper stick-on heart, no more than half an inch wide.

"What is that supposed to cover?" I asked. "And do you have any bigger ones?"

She laughed as if she thought I was trying to be funny. "You put it on your arm. Then, when you get out you can see how tanned you are!"

She said that the door on the chamber was automatic, that when I approached it would open, and once I was inside with my feet on the two metal plates, it would close. Then she left me to my fate.

After about the fifteenth time of making sure the door to the room was locked, I got undressed and approached the capsule. Nothing happened. I tried approaching it from several angles. Nothing.

In exasperation, I decided to quit. But the moment I bent over to pick up my jeans, the door opened. So I dived inside. Feeling like Captain Kirk ("Beam me up, Scotty!"), I stood with my feet on the two plates and waited for something to happen.

Suddenly a disembodied voice began to count down: "five-four-three-two-one"!

If you have never had the experience of a spray tan, it's hard to explain what it's like to be sandblasted with the tanning solution. Suffice it to say, even though one is shocked by the initial blast, it would be better not to open one's mouth and yell. I know that . . . now!

After I had been fully soaked, the frontal assault stopped and the same robotic voice encouraged me to turn around so that I could be properly basted. Finally, the ordeal was over. As I loped out of my chamber, dripping with brown goop, I saw Barry's card lying on my chair. *May all your dreams come true.* All I could think was this was not quite what I had in mind!

Ever been there? Oh, I don't mean the tanning chamber (which actually did a pretty nice job). I mean, have you ever had a situation where life just did not turn out as you imagined it would? A situation where you asked yourself why? All kidding aside, I know I have. And I know others who have. It's no laughing matter. To the contrary, disappointment can often lead to depression and disillusionment.

It even caused John the Baptist to question his whole life . . .

ARE YOU THE ONE?

Jesus called John the last and greatest of all the prophets. That is quite an amazing statement. But then again, there are many things about John's birth and life that are remarkable. It all began when the angel Gabriel appeared to Zacharias the priest and his wife, Elizabeth, and told them that although they were old and Elizabeth was unable to have children, they were going to have a child.

Don't fear, Zachariah. Your prayer has been heard. Elizabeth, your wife, will bear a son by you. You are to name him John. You're going to leap like a gazelle for joy, and not only you—many will delight in his birth. He'll achieve great stature with God.

He'll drink neither wine nor beer. He'll be filled with the Holy Spirit from the moment he leaves his mother's womb. He will turn many sons and daughters of Israel back to their God. He will herald God's arrival in the style and strength of Elijah, soften the hearts of parents to children, and kindle devout understanding among hardened skeptics—he'll get the people ready for God. (Luke 1:13–17 MSG)

The mention of the prophet Elijah would have huge significance for Zachariah. The prophet Malachi had foretold that Elijah would return before God's promised one: "But also look ahead: I'm sending Elijah the prophet to clear the way for the Big Day of GOD—the decisive Judgment Day!" (Malachi 4:5 MSG). These were the closing words recorded in the Old Testament before a long period of about four hundred years of silence.

Then God began speaking again. Everything was about to change.

From the moment John left his mother's womb, he was filled with the Holy Spirit. He lived a very monastic life in the desert and spent his time preparing for his divine mission—the moment when he would see the Spirit of God descend like a dove upon the Messiah. He had no knowledge of who the promised Messiah was until he saw the Spirit of God descend and heard a voice from heaven announcing Jesus was indeed God's beloved Son.

John must have been surprised. He and Jesus were related; they were second cousins. The sign was clear, however, and so he announced, "Behold! The Lamb of God who takes away the sin of the world!" (John 1:29 NKJV).

Jesus' ministry began to take off, and crowds followed him. I imagine part of the reason for the switch was that his message and style were very different from John's. John was blunt and confrontational; he wasn't out to win popularity awards. On one occasion, when he saw some Pharisees and Sadducees who had shown up for a baptism, John turned on them and said, "Brood of snakes! What do you think you're doing slithering down here to the river? Do you think a little water on your snakeskins is going to make any difference?" (Matthew 3:7 MSG). And as the months passed, many of those who'd once followed John and listened to his teaching now followed Jesus.

Some might have expected John to be jealous. But when his disciples pointed out the defections to him, John only told them this was how it was supposed to be—Jesus was to increase in popularity and power, and John was to decrease (John 3:30).

But life for John was about to take a sharp left turn. He would soon find himself in a place he could never have imagined. And then the questions would begin to churn inside his soul.

King Herod was the regional ruler at this time, and he had married his brother's wife, in violation of Old Testament law. John was very outspoken about the matter and publicly called Herod an adulterer.

Herod's wife, Herodias, was infuriated at John's accusation and asked Herod to arrest John for daring to speak out against her. Herod did so but was afraid to execute someone considered a man of God. He knew John was popular with the common people.

But one night at a party, the opportunity presented itself to

Herod—on a platter, so to speak. It was his birthday and Salome, his stepdaughter (and niece!), danced for his guests. Herod was very drunk and told Salome to ask for anything at all as a gift for dancing. She asked her mother, Herodias, what she should ask for. Herodias was quick to tell her to ask for the head of John the Baptist.

Well, that sobered Herod up pretty quickly, but he had already given his word. John would have to die.

But what had been happening to John as he sat in his prison cell? Probably not what we'd expect of such a devoted prophet of God. The Bible says, "And John, calling two of his disciples to him, sent them to Jesus, saying, 'Are You the Coming One, or do we look for another?'" (Luke 7:19 NKJV).

This passage of Scripture has had a huge impact on my life. It affects how I pray and the window through which I see my life. The reason the words affect me is this: of all people to ask Jesus if he was the Messiah, I would never have expected John the Baptist to question him. That is, until I took a closer look. It's my fervent prayer that as you take a look into the dark night of this amazing servant's soul, you will find strength and hope in the midst of your questions. Not only that, I pray you will see that Christ has great compassion on those who question from an honest heart.

Have you ever prayed and prayed for an answer and not recognized it when it was sent? I know I have. And apparently John did as well. You see, Jesus did not behave as John thought Israel's Messiah would. Jesus wasn't out toppling the Roman government and ushering in a new era. He wasn't living the austere life, exhorting the people to change. Instead, he was wandering the nearby towns telling stories! His friends were loud, uncouth fishermen and reformed tax collectors. They went to parties and drank wine at weddings.

As John sat in Herod's bleak dungeon, he must have reflected on his life and wondered how he had ended up in such a place. I'm sure he was discouraged—as you well know, the enemy loves to taunt and lie to God's people when they are already down. John wondered if he had gotten it all wrong. Had he spent his whole life for nothing, and was the Messiah still to come?

That question must have haunted him. John was the one who was supposed to prepare the way for the Messiah. What if he had publicly identified the wrong man?

We read John's story in context of the whole canon of Scripture. We see the role he played and what Jesus said about him. And we assume, "Well, yes, that's all as it was supposed to be." But remember, John lived and died before the crucifixion and resurrection. He never got to see the promise fulfilled. And there, in the dungeon, he doubted.

Jesus sent an answer back to John:

> The blind see,
> The lame walk,
> Lepers are cleansed,
> The deaf hear,
> The dead are raised,
> The wretched of the earth have God's salvation hospitality
>   extended to them.
> (Luke 7:21–23 MSG)

Jesus was paraphrasing from a messianic passage in Isaiah 35. He told John's disciples to tell him the miracles the Messiah would perform were going to happen just a few miles from his prison cell.

I wonder if John found the answer comforting or ironic. Did it soothe his weary heart or rub salt into an open wound? One of the promises about the coming Messiah was that he would set the captives free, and yet John now sat in prison about to be beheaded on the apparent whim of a dancing girl and a bitter mother.

And yet there was more—a little phrase tacked on to the end of Jesus' message to John that is easy to miss, yet says so much: "And blessed is he who is not offended because of Me" (Luke 7:23 NKJV).

What an interesting message to send back to this man Jesus loved dearly. In essence he was saying, "John, will you still love and serve a God you do not understand? Will you place your head down on the execution block still seeing through a glass darkly? Will you still worship even though you have questions? Will you still love me when my answers are not what you expected? If you can do this, your reward will be great."

TRUSTING IN THE DARKNESS

I don't imagine John received much comfort or warmth during his life. Remember, he had been set apart from before birth. He never married or had children. He never knew what it was to have his own child's tender arms around his neck or little face snuggled up to his cheek. He lived a life of denial because he knew he had been chosen by God.

I imagine life was not always easy for John, and I'm sure he looked at Jesus and wondered about both their callings. And pondered what had brought him to this state of events.

Yet when the prison guards took John away and he realized he had but moments to live, John took his final steps trusting in God in the darkness. Yes, he would serve a God he didn't understand. Yes, he would place his head on the execution block. Yes, he would worship and love his Lord no matter what.

The whole thing is deeply moving! I love John's faith. But even more so, I love to think of how it must have been after Jesus ascended to heaven and reached out with nail-pierced hands to take the hand of his beloved friend John the Baptist. Blessed indeed!

Remember that on those days when you find yourself questioning, as John did. When you wonder why you pray at all. When you feel as if what you don't know far exceeds what you do know. Remember we are called to walk by faith and not by sight because so much of the truth we seek lives in the invisible world. One day we will know even as we are known. But until then, as John did, we take the next step and the next one after that.

When Jesus' disciples told him that John had been beheaded, Jesus got into a boat and went off by himself. I believe in those moments his heart broke for John—just as it does for us when life does not turn out as we expected and God does not answer our prayers as we thought he would.

But Jesus said, "Blessed is he [or she] who is not offended because of Me" (Luke 7:23 NKJV). Jesus blessed John for his belief. And he will bless us as well. We just have to continue in faith.

This doesn't mean we won't at times question ourselves and God. And that's okay. I think John's life tells us that asking questions is all right; it is a mark of trust and relationship. When John's disciples told Jesus what John was asking, Jesus was not offended. And he will not be offended by our questions either. So wherever you are today, know that you can ask the hard questions. The "why?" questions. And the "who-what-when-and-where?" questions too.

Remember, though, that in the end the only answer that matters is that, yes, Jesus is the One! Sometimes our Father does not give us the answer we want, but he always gives us his Son. If we can remember that—if we can keep loving him even when our hearts are uncertain or broken—we will be blessed.

"Lord, I believe: help Thou mine unbelief";
Let me no other master know but Thee.
Thou art the Christian's God, the only King and Chief
Of all who soldiers of the cross would be.

"Lord, I believe," in mercy grant me grace
To know Thee, blessèd Savior, more and more;
I can do naught without Thee; Jesus, show Thy face
Unto Thy servant who would Thee adore.

"Lord, I believe"; the hold of sin is strong,
And stout its heart to pluck me from Thy love;
But stronger is Thy grace; oh, strengthen and prolong
The work of faith in me, my doubts remove.

"Lord, I believe: help Thou mine unbelief";
Be this my prayer though good report and ill;
Only to Thee I cling; if long my day or brief,
Master and Savior, I will trust Thee still!
—DAVID H. HOWARD

(12)

Are You Asking Me to Let Go?

Falling Forward

Every tomorrow has two handles. We can take hold of it with the handle of
anxiety or the handle of faith. —Henry Ward Beecher

God who made you has something to say to you;
   the God who formed you in the womb wants to help you.
Don't be afraid, dear servant Jacob,
   Jeshurun, the one I chose.
For I will pour water on the thirsty ground
   and send streams coursing through the parched earth.
I will pour my Spirit into your descendants
   and my blessing on your children.
They shall sprout like grass on the prairie,
   like willows alongside creeks.
—Isaiah 44:2–4 msg

Christian didn't learn to walk until he was about eighteen months
old. This seemed to alarm some of my friends, but it didn't worry
me at all. He could crawl at the speed of a BMW, and I intuitively
knew as his mother that when he was ready to walk, he would walk.

147

He's been that way with almost everything new he's learned. For instance, when it was within the time frame for getting out of diapers, I asked Christian if he wanted to do so. He said he did not, but he would let me know when he was ready.

One day we were at McDonald's with one of his friends, who was a year older than Christian. His friend said he needed to use the restroom, so we all marched in. Christian must have noticed that his friend didn't have a diaper on.

On the car ride home after dropping his buddy off, he announced, "I'm done with diapers, Mom!" He never wore one again.

It was the same with his faith journey. When he was five years old, I got a little book from Campus Crusade for Christ that explained simply but clearly to a child what it means to ask Jesus to be your Savior. I let him take a look at the pages and then he asked me to read it to him. I read it through twice (he called for an encore) and then asked him what he thought. He told me it sounded like a very good thing to do, but he was not ready yet.

About two weeks later, he asked me if I still had the book. I told him I did and at his request read it through again. Then he said, "I'm ready, Mom. Would you pray with me?"

If I had to write down what the highlights of my life are, that prayer would be at the top of my list. There is nothing—absolutely nothing—that could mean more to me or to Barry than to know that our son has his own relationship with Jesus Christ. It's a reminder that Christian is becoming more independent from us—and more dependent on God. A bittersweet but wonderful changing of the guard.

LEARNING TO LIVE

The stages of a child's life are marked by joy and sorrow, struggle and laughter, falling down and getting back up again. Being a parent is the most demanding endeavor I have ever embraced. I have never encountered a greater challenge in my own prayer life than in relation to my son. At times I find it hard to know where the lines are. As a mom, God expects me to care for Christian and nurture him and protect him as much as I can. But the other reality is that he is God's child, and I am called to daily relinquish him to our Father. At times he will fall, and I have to trust that when he falls, he will fall forward into the arms that reach where I can't go. As he grows, the challenges increase and the call for trust is heralded in my heart.

As I write, Christian is ten years old and about to graduate from elementary to middle school. (In Christian's school system, middle school begins with fifth grade.) At this stage and age Barry and I see ourselves as life coaches, side by side with our boy, helping him to make good choices and to take responsibility for poor ones. We work hard to help him develop good study habits that will serve him well later in life, to make friends worth keeping, and to be respectful of authority. We instruct him on the value of money, saving and spending, and giving back to God what is his. We teach him to understand the value of each human life—that every man, woman, and child is loved by God and deserves to be treated with kindness and respect—and that he has a right to God-given boundaries no one should cross or challenge.

So many lessons—no wonder the poor child is exhausted!

When it comes to faith, though, at some point Christian will have to forget everything he learned from us and fall into the arms of God. What a paradox! From the moment our children are born, we prepare them to become independent. We teach them to walk by themselves and make good decisions on their own so that at some point they can go off and make their own lives. But when it comes to a relationship with God, there is a part of them (and us) that will always be called to be a child—to be willing to trust what cannot be seen and step out at times into the darkness listening only for the sound of their Father's voice.

One of my dearest friends in the world is Sandi Patty. She and her brothers were raised by their lovely parents in Phoenix, Arizona. They lived in a little house, and one of the fun games they played as children was with Sandi's dad. She wrote about it in her book *Falling Forward*.[1]

The game was that her father would put each one of the kids up onto the roof (don't worry—it wasn't terribly high) and they would jump into his arms. It looked fun to Sandi until it was her turn, and then she froze on the edge of the roof. What had seemed very doable as she watched her brothers jump now seemed terrifying.

Sandi's dad said to her, "Sandi, one way or another, you are going to fall. If you fall backward, there is nothing I can do to help you. But if you fall forward, I will catch you."

This simple lesson has stayed with Sandi through years of tremendous success and years of heartache. In 2007, she was a guest speaker with Women of Faith. As she shared her story of finding herself in some very dark and scary places, she remembered her father's words—which now became the words of her heavenly Father: "Sandi, fall forward, and I will catch you."

I hear those words clearly as a call to the prayer of surrendering:

"Father, I am falling forward into your arms." Why is that so hard for us as believers to do? Why is it so hard to pray, "Not my will but yours, God"? At least I know it's hard for me. What about you? Do you find, like me, that although you know you should give a situation to God, you just can't quite let go? That although there's something you know God is laying on your heart, you're too afraid to commit to it?

There's a strong instinct in every human soul to want to understand everything and know what we are saying yes to. When ethicist John Kavanaugh spent three months in Calcutta with Mother Teresa at "the house of the dying," she asked him how she might serve him. He asked for her prayers. She asked him what he wanted her to pray for, and he said, "For clarity." She replied, "No, I will not do that. Clarity is the last thing you are clinging to and you must let go of it."[2]

It's hard to take our hands off the things we long to "fix" and trust God to do what only he can do. Or give in even when we're scared of the outcome. To some, the rewards might not seem worth it. But if we cannot allow our prayer life to reflect our absolute belief in God's will in our lives, we're never really committing to him, are we?

Perhaps you have seen the charming movie *Waking Ned Devine*. Set in Ireland, this story is about a man who wins the lottery. Unfortunately he has just died, and his friends are trying to find a way to trick the lottery representative into believing one of them is Ned. It's a very funny tale, but it's the honesty of a young character that stuck with me for some time after seeing it.

There is a scene in the movie when a ten-year-old boy questions the interim pastor of the village church about his faith. He asks the minister if he ever gets to see God personally. The minister replies that he does not, although on occasion he gets "revelations."

Not satisfied with that answer, the boy presses on. He asks if the pastor's job pays well, and the minister has to admit that most of his rewards are spiritual rather than financial.

Curious about the boy's questions, the minister asks him if he is considering a life of service to God. The boy replies, "Not really. I don't want to work for someone I never see and who doesn't even pay minimum wage."

Welcome to the life of faith—although it is my experience that God is no man or woman's debtor! Really, though, what the minister was trying to convey to the boy was what it looks like to live with mystery, to live a life of relinquishment. There is nothing more freeing than praying with absolute submission. Because letting go is the catalyst for change.

I didn't used to be a huge fan of the word *relinquishment*— mainly because when you look at synonyms for the word you find *give up, surrender, abandon, hand over*. My struggle for so many years was because of a deep-rooted fear in my life: what would happen if I prayed to God and told him I was really letting go of all the things I "control" (home, work, marriage, parenting, etc.)?

But I've come to realize my focus was in the wrong place and I was asking the wrong question. The right focus is on the heart and character of God, and the right question is, "Whom are we being asked to relinquish our lives to?"

That changes everything. It changes *us*. In ways we might never experience if we didn't fall forward.

Just ask the apostle Peter. The prayer of relinquishment, of finally coming to understand that he was not in control, reshaped his life.

STEP OUT OF THE BOAT!

In many ways, Peter was the spokesman for the twelve disciples. He is the most quoted of them in the four gospel narratives. And he played a key role in three events that marked the transition from Old Testament life to New Testament revelation.

In Matthew 16, Peter was the first to openly declare Jesus was the Christ. It happened in Caesarea Philippi. Jesus asked his disciples what people were saying about him and who they said he was. They told him that some said Jesus was Elijah or one of the other prophets. Herod was terrified that Jesus was a resurrected John the Baptist, come to seek revenge for his beheading, and so that rumor was also circulating.

Then Jesus asked his friends, "But who do you say that I am?"

Peter answered, "You are the Christ, the Son of the living God" (Matthew 16:15–16 NKJV). This declaration by Peter was a prayer of confession and adoration, though it may not have seemed that way to Peter.

After this declaration, there is a shift in Christ's teaching—from concentrating on the kingdom to centering on the cross.

Peter played an important role in other key moments too. His sermon on the day of pentecost led to the formation of the early church. As he spoke, he revealed his new understanding of how Christ taught him to pray during the Sermon on the Mount. He declared the kingdom of God, gave glory to God, and invited the listeners to confess their sins and be saved. His visit with the Roman centurion Cornelius was the first time that the doors of the church were opened to those outside the Jewish family. This one act was a true falling forward in faith and prayer. God asked

Peter to step outside what he understood to be true and trust. The Jewish believers who embraced Christ knew their Messiah had come, but now Peter was being asked to step off this narrow ledge and trust that God had a wider platform for him to stand on.

This radical faith and leadership did not happen overnight. Peter's growth in maturity was bathed in tears and failure, with falling down and rising up again. He began as a simple fisherman, became a disciple, then a preacher, and finally a missionary. But before he was able to do any of this, before he was able to stand and speak out his love and devotion for Christ, Peter fell forward.

You might remember the story in Matthew 14:22–33. Matthew is the only gospel writer who records it. I think it must have had quite an impact on him because Matthew was with the disciples and Peter, and he saw it firsthand. It was nighttime, and they were all in a boat. Jesus was not with them. He had stayed on the other side of the shore to dismiss the crowd after the miracle of feeding five thousand men and twice as many women and children. Then he had gone up to the mountain to be alone with his Father. (I can only assume that after each miracle, each time that heaven broke into earth's reality, Christ was exhausted and drained and so he wanted to be alone with his Father.)

The disciples were having some difficulty in their rented boat. They were about three miles out into the Sea of Galilee and were fighting a strong wind. Then, at the fourth watch of the night, which would be between three and six in the morning, the disciples saw a strange figure approach the boat.

The Greek word used here is *phantasma*, which means "phantom" or "apparition." The disciples were terrified by this apparition who appeared to be walking on top of the water. They thought it had to be a ghost.

But the figure called out to them and told them not to be afraid. *Wait,* they thought. *Is that . . . Jesus?*

The moon disappeared behind clouds. It was hard to see, and waves splashed against the side of the boat. So Peter called out to Jesus and said, "Lord, if it really is you, ask me to come to you."

Jesus said, "Come."

Peter stepped over the side of the boat and placed his foot on top of one of the waves they had been battling all night. His faith was high. After all, he had just witnessed Jesus take a boy's lunch and feed a multitude of people.

And now he was doing it; he was actually walking across the waves! He could see Jesus with his arms outstretched, so he took another step . . . and another.

But a wave splashed against him, and for a moment Peter took his eyes off Jesus. The seen world became much more vivid in that moment than the unseen, and as Peter panicked, he began to sink. He called out to Jesus to save him, and the Lord of the waves reached out and caught his friend. The moment that Jesus stepped into the boat, the sea settled down in submission.

Peter learned a lesson that night: that the only true catalyst for a positive change is falling forward and relinquishing ourselves to God's care. When he was able to do this, he went from mere fisherman to one of the greatest and most godly mentors we have today.

It didn't happen overnight. As the Bible tells us, sanctification is a process. Just like Sandi standing on the roofline, Peter faced his fears on the waves. But the day he tried to blend in with a hostile crowd outside the home of the high priest, he had other fears to face.

TURNING BACK TO JESUS

It was inconceivable to Peter what had taken place in the last few hours. It was as if he had watched sand running through his hands and he couldn't stop it. Everything he knew to be true about himself now seemed to be a lie. He was strong and fearless, but now his stomach and heart were gripped by fear. It was as if everyone around him seemed larger than life, threatening and menacing. There was evil in the air that night, in a way Peter had never experienced before.

Mark 14:66–72 records Peter's dark struggle with fear. He stood among the crowd of those who had gathered to watch Jesus' trial in the house of the high priest. Someone turned to him and, with eyes that bore through his soul and tried to pull him into this death net, said, "You are one of his friends!"

"No!" Peter insisted.

"I've seen you with him," hissed another.

"No!" Peter said again.

"You can't hide here—we see you!" they accused.

"No! I don't even know him!"

No! No! No! Three such small words, and yet for Peter they carried the weight of the world. Thankfully, after initially running away from God that night, Peter turned around and ran toward him. He fell forward, back into the arms of his loving Father.

I think in that way Peter's experience was a gift. Strange though that sounds, I believe God in his mercy helped Peter understand that he needed to lean on God—that he wasn't strong enough to withstand the external battles or internal fears on his own. Once Peter had that clear, he was ready for all that lay ahead on his new path. He was ready to stand and speak to a hostile and volatile crowd on the day of pentecost. He was ready to face opposition as he took the gospel outside the walls of Jerusalem and began a missionary journey that led to you and to me.

And to our own "falling forward" journey of faith, I think being asked to trust is sometimes like having a mirror held up in front of us, giving us an opportunity to see what is really true about ourselves. When we face those things that make it difficult to trust, we are invited to fall forward in prayer into the arms of the one who waits to catch and strengthen us.

When Christian starts to play football this year, he will hear from his coach what every kid his age does: "When you fall—and you will fall—fall forward and make the most of the play." It is wisdom not only when you are on the field or on the roof but when you stand at the edge of an unknown moment in life. We have a Father who stands above and below all the scary places of our lives. He stands with arms open wide to catch us when we fall. So fall forward!

All to Jesus, I surrender;
All to Him I freely give;
I will ever love and trust Him,
In His presence daily live.

I surrender all, I surrender all,
All to Thee, my blessèd Savior,
I surrender all.

All to Jesus I surrender;
Humbly at His feet I bow,
Worldly pleasures all forsaken;
Take me, Jesus, take me now.

All to Jesus, I surrender;
Make me, Savior, wholly Thine;
Let me feel the Holy Spirit,
Truly know that Thou art mine.

All to Jesus, I surrender;
Lord, I give myself to Thee;
Fill me with Thy love and power;
Let Thy blessing fall on me.

All to Jesus I surrender;
Now I feel the sacred flame.
O the joy of full salvation!
Glory, glory, to His Name!
—JUDSON W. VAN DEVENTER

part 4

the
purpose

13

Lay Your Burdens Down

The Gift of Confession

Tears are like blood in the wounds of the soul. —Gregory of Nyssa

Create in me a pure heart, O God, and renew a steadfast spirit within me.
Do not cast me from your presence or take your Holy Spirit from me.
Restore to me the joy of your salvation and grant me a willing spirit,
to sustain me. —Psalm 51:10–12

I love to watch a good movie, but I have very little time to go to a
movie theater. (I think the last movie I bought a ticket for had
Charlie Chaplin in it!) But as modern technology has marched on,
that is not a problem. I can go to a rental store and get a movie or
have it delivered to my door. I can download one onto my video
iPod or onto my laptop.

I am grateful for the convenience of such things, but for certain
movies nothing takes the place of the big screen. For me, the Lord
of the Rings trilogy fits that category. (I got to watch them on an
IMAX screen. Wow!)

Another movie made for theaters is *The Mission*. If you have
not seen it before, put this book down right now and go and rent

it—it's glorious. (The movie gets a bit bloody at the end as some of the South American Indians are slaughtered, so if that is something you can't handle, watch it until the last ten minutes!)

Based on a true story, *The Mission* is about the experiences of a Jesuit missionary in eighteenth-century South America. Father Gabriel, played brilliantly by Jeremy Irons, enters the South American jungle to build a mission and convert a community of Guarani Indians to Christianity. The mission and the territory of the Guarani tribe used to be under Spanish authority but has been handed over to the Portuguese, who do not trust the Indians and intend to wipe them out. Rodrigo Mendoza, a reformed Portuguese mercenary played with intensity and angst by Robert De Niro, joins Father Gabriel to help protect the tribe from these colonials.

I was most touched by De Niro's character, Mendoza. As the story unfolds, it becomes clear why Mendoza is there. He sees the Jesuit mission as a sanctuary and a place of forgiveness for the murder of his brother, whom he killed over a woman. A former slave trader who cared little for human life, he is now consumed by guilt. At first he tries to brush it off and push the pain under the surface, but he can't. His life is stuck in limbo, as he has nowhere to take the guilt.

What I most appreciate about the portrayal of this weight of guilt and shame is that we are given a physical picture of a spiritual reality. To access the mission, it is necessary to climb up a very steep mountain. Whenever Father Gabriel has to make the climb from the river to the mission, the Guarani Indians carry his baggage and help him find footholds and what rock to grasp next. They are used to the climb and are very lithe and limber.

Mendoza refuses to let anyone help him. He struggles to climb the mountain with his bags tied to his back. Time after time he falls back down the mountainside and the sharp rocks cut into his flesh. With tears running down his face, he starts all over again.

When he finally makes it to the top, one of the Indians takes a knife and cuts his burden off his back. He looks into the face of Mendoza and starts to laugh. He laughs and laughs and finally Mendoza joins him, and they laugh till Mendoza's tears of pain and guilt are replaced by tears of joy and relief.

A PICTURE OF REPENTANCE

In this one scene is the picture of sin, guilt, and the gift offered to everyone who will prayerfully bring their burden to Christ in true repentance and allow him to take it from them. The picture can be broken down into four steps:

- Sinning and feeling the weight of the sin
- Grieving the sin
- Trying to personally atone for the sin
- Having your sin taken from you

Each of these steps matters, so let's break them down.

Step One: Sinning and Feeling the Weight of the Sin

Have you ever been in a situation where you know what you are about to do is wrong but you do it anyway? Afterward it can feel as if the weight of the world is on your shoulders. The compulsion that drove you to take the step has left you with a sickening emptiness. The psalmist, who has given us a handbook on repentance and confession, writes:

> When I kept silent, my bones grew old
> Through my groaning all the day long.
> For day and night Your hand was heavy upon me;
> My vitality was turned into the drought of summer.
> I acknowledged my sin to You,
> And my iniquity I have not hidden.
> I said, "I will confess my transgressions to the LORD,"
> And You forgave the iniquity of my sin. (Psalm 32:3–5 NKJV)

According to this psalm, when David tried to minimize his sin or ignore it, he became physically ill. Because he refused to confess, he suffered. God has designed us to live transparent lives, and when we try to push our stuff deep down inside rather than come before God in prayer, it can affect our physical health and certainly our emotional and spiritual health. Not to mention our prayer life itself. Prayer is God's gift to us as we live in human flesh. It is where we can and should unload the stuff that weighs us down.

When I was about Christian's age, I took some money from my mom's wallet. It wasn't very much, but she noticed it was missing. She asked my sister, my brother, and me if we had taken it. We all said no. Now I had added lying to my pile. Mom concluded she must have misplaced it, and the day moved on for everyone apart from me.

I cannot describe how that unconfessed sin gnawed at me. That night I tried to sleep, but as I lay in bed, I felt physically sick. I also felt that there was a wall between my mom and me. She was not aware of it, but I was.

Finally I had to get up and tell her what I had done and ask her to forgive me. She forgave me. There were consequences for my stealing and lying, but they were sweet compared to the burden that had been on my back all day.

There is a sense of "rightness" when we come to God in prayer, confess our sin, and own it. There is relief in telling the truth. But sin is characterized not only by the outward action we take but by our inner attitudes as well. I think these attitudes are potentially far more devastating to the human heart and spirit, as unforgiveness and bitterness eat at the soul. Medical science now acknowledges a clear link between emotional health and physical health. When we refuse to forgive someone who has wounded us, that unforgiveness is like a stone in our spirits. Like the baggage that Mendoza attempted to drag up the side of the mountain, the weight of unforgiveness causes us to fall backward. We can pray all we want, but if we're not going anywhere emotionally, chances are our prayers aren't either.

It is well noted in many medical studies that there is a relationship between what is going on in our soul and spirit and what is happening with our physical health. Negative emotions such as anger, unforgiveness, and anxiety can adversely affect not only our prayer life but our physical health. Conversely, positive emotions such as humor and hope can serve to improve health and increase longevity . . . and our joyful, grateful prayer life.

Step Two: Grieving the Sin

This next step is one most of us would admit we are in tune with. But I wonder if we've forgotten what it looks like to biblically grieve for our sins. The Greek word for a broken and a contrite heart is *penthos*. It translates also as "inward godly sorrow." As Richard Foster writes in his book *Prayer*, it is "the Prayer of Tears."[1]

There is a world of difference between feeling guilty and being repentant. When Christian was in third grade, he and three of his friends carried out what they described as a "science project" in the boys' restroom. They tried to see how many paper towels they could stuff into one commode and then they flushed it. Obviously (and I'm not even good at science!) the toilet overflowed and water poured everywhere. Christian and his cohorts were sent to the principal's office.

This was horrifying to Christian, who had never been in so much trouble before. The principal told them how selfish and irresponsible they had been and then gave each boy chores to do to help the poor janitor who had to clean up their mess. Barry and I added our own punishment by banning Christian's computer use for the week.

When he was tucked in bed that night, I talked to him about the experience and what his thoughts were.

He said, "I cried twice, Mom."

"Why did you cry twice?" I asked.

"I cried once when I was caught, and then I cried again when I saw how much work we had given the janitor. He is such a nice man."

Christian's first tears were for himself, his second for what his "experiment" had cost someone else. I was deeply grateful for this experience in Christian's life—that at such an early age he was able to understand sin has consequences beyond our own lives. He worked side by side with that sweet man all week, and I honestly think he enjoyed every minute.

I believe that the depth to which we feel the weight of our sin and prayerfully repent with tears will be the depth to which we experience the true joy that only a believer can know. Sometimes in our prayer lives we don't get past the first tears. But it's crucial that we do.

An indication of how deep our repentance runs is how our behavior changes after our confession. The Greek word for repentance is *metanoia*. *Meta* means "change" and *noia* means "mind." We can't just be sorrowful for the situation and consequences; we need to repent and literally change directions in our thoughts about right and wrong.

When Peter spoke to the crowd on the day of pentecost, he told them it was our sin that nailed Jesus to the cross. As they began to grasp what Peter was saying, "they were *cut to the heart* and said to Peter and the other apostles, 'Brothers, what shall we do?'" (Acts 2:37; emphasis added). The indication that the repentance was real was that they changed how they were living and lived a different way. They were cut to the heart by their sin and what it had cost Christ.

To us it's the difference between praying, "God, I'm so sorry for my actions. Please forgive me," and continuing with, "And, Lord, show me how I might act differently in the future, because I don't want to be the same person I was before." How often have we forgotten this crucial step in confession? I am a huge fan of God's grace. The unmerited favor of God is a gift I have no words for, but I wonder if too often I hurry off to grace before sitting for a while with the prayer of tears.

Scripture is full of examples of those who loved God and who soaked their beds with tears, not only for their sins, but for the sins of the people.

-> "I am weary with my groaning; all night I make my bed
swim; I drench my couch with my tears. My eye wastes
away because of grief" (Psalm 6:6–7 NKJV).

-> "Make Your face shine upon Your servant, and teach me
Your statutes. Rivers of water run down from my eyes,
because men do not keep Your law" (Psalm 119:135–36
NKJV).

-> ". . . who, in the days of His flesh, when He had offered
up prayers and supplications, with vehement cries and
tears to Him who was able to save Him from death, and
was heard because of His godly fear" (Hebrews 5:7 NKJV).

-> "You know, from the first day that I came to Asia, in what
manner I always lived among you, serving the Lord with
all humility, with many tears and trials" (Acts 20:18–19
NKJV).

Step Three: Trying to Personally Atone for the Sin

This is a hard one—it's heartbreaking, really. I'm thinking of the
number of people who sit in isolation, feeling unworthy of life and
love. I'm thinking of those who drink themselves to sleep at night
or are addicted to pain medication or drugs, trying to fill a void
inside they would struggle to put a name to. For many it is a deep
sense of shame and guilt with no source to attach it to and
nowhere to take it. They try to atone for what they have done, but
since they're uncertain of its basis, their efforts never feel like
enough. And because of it, their prayers for forgiveness—if indeed
they can even pray—seem pointless.

I spent most of my life trying to atone for whatever was wrong with me—thousands of prayers begging God to forgive and fix me. I, too, would have been unable to put a name to why I felt the way I did. All I knew was that at the very essence of my being I felt like there was something wrong with me. I thought if anyone got too close to me, they wouldn't like what they saw.

As a child, I observed the change in my father after his cerebral hemorrhage. He was now paralyzed on one side and unable to speak, but we still found ways of communicating. As his deterioration continued, his personality was affected. He would at one moment be loving and kind and then angry and unpredictable. Children are the best absorbers of information but the least equipped to interpret the events they witness. In my mind, if my father now seemed to hate me, then I must have done something wrong; I just didn't know what.

After one particularly alarming episode when my father tried to bring his cane down on my skull, he was taken to a psychiatric hospital where he died. I was left with a huge hole in my heart and a question that rumbled in the basement of my soul for many years: "What is wrong with me?"

Even though I gave my life to Christ at eleven, I was thirty-four years old before I let him cut the burden off my back and watch it tumble down the mountainside. The month I spent in a psychiatric ward for my depression was the first time I faced everything I believed to be true about myself. I had nothing left to hide behind and no energy left to run. And I realized I had spent most of my years in ministry trying to atone for whatever was "wrong" with me. Trying and failing. No prayer I prayed was ever enough to outweigh what I felt inside.

The trouble with the kind of deep shame we are unable to put into words is that we sit alone with it instead of taking it to our Father in prayer. If you have ever struggled with this, I want to suggest a couple of things that might be helpful. First, I encourage you to make your very questions and lack of understanding a matter of prayer:

> Father,
>
> I have such a deep sense of unworthiness. I feel that at the very core of my being there is something wrong with me. Please help me to understand why I am struggling this way. Please lead me to the right person to talk to and the right passages of Scripture to study.

Second, I encourage you to talk with someone you believe is trustworthy—a pastor or Christian counselor or wise friend. Ask that person to join you in prayer that God will walk you through this journey.

Perhaps one of the saddest accounts of someone trying to atone for their own sins is Judas, the betrayer of Christ. His remorse and inability to make up for his sin cost him his life at his own hands:

> When Judas, who had betrayed him, saw that Jesus was condemned, he was seized with remorse and returned the thirty silver coins to the chief priests and the elders. "I have sinned," he said, "for I have betrayed innocent blood."
>
> "What is that to us?" they replied. "That's your responsibility."
>
> So Judas threw the money into the temple and left. Then he went away and hanged himself. (Matthew 27:3–5)

No matter how hard we try to pay for our sins on our own— no matter how long we try to personally atone for them—it will never be enough. We'll never be able to fully purge our guilt and our feelings of inadequacy. No amount of begging, suffering, or self-hate can do the job. There is only One who can take away the sin. We need a Savior.

Step Four: Having Your Sin Taken from You

I will never forget the day I was drenched in tears at the foot of the cross, and I felt the love of God reach out and cut my burden from my back. I had spent two weeks in the hospital facing every ounce of the shame that had weighed me down for years. It was over-whelming, and just like Mendoza, I was exhausted. Unlike me, Mendoza was weighed down by guilt for a crime he had commit-ted, but I discovered that whether we have picked up the burden of shame ourselves or had it placed there by another, the weight is the same.

I asked the doctor if I could have a three-hour pass to go to church. He agreed, and a young nurse took me. We sat in the back row of a small church in Washington, D.C. The fall sun-light streamed through the stained-glass windows, and I felt as if I was on holy ground. I listened as the pastor said (and I para-phrase from memory): "Some of you here today feel as if you are dead inside. You can already feel the earth being heaped upon your casket. But Jesus is here! You don't even have to get yourself out of the pit. Just reach out your hand, and he will grasp hold of you."

I have never walked to the front of a church before, but that morning I ran to the altar and lay on my face at the foot of the cross.

The words of an old hymn went through my mind: "Nothing in my hands I bring, simply to thy cross I cling."

As I lay there with tears pouring down my cheeks, I felt more loved than I had ever felt in my life. I felt like a child who had been lost and suddenly scooped up into the arms of her father. I understood Mendoza's laughter when the native cut away his belongings from his back, because when you have been carrying something for so long and suddenly, in a moment, it is gone, you are filled with tears and holy laughter.

To finally and completely pray for, accept, and confess the truth of all that Jesus did for us on the cross is a simply marvelous feeling. As Bernard of Clairvaux described it:

To shame our sins He blushed in blood;
He closed his eyes to show us God;
Let all the world fall down and know
That none but God such love can show.

Confession is a gift from God. It is a gift of grace and mercy in a broken world. To feel the depth of joy God wants for his children, we have to feel the weight of our sin and grieve what it cost him. But we cannot lose ourselves in the pain and regret and feelings of unworthiness. Instead, like Rodrigo Mendoza, we can look into the face of our deliverer and laugh as our burden rolls away.

At the cross, at the cross where I first saw the light,
And the burden of my heart rolled away,
It was there by faith I received my sight,
And now I am happy all the day!

Thy body slain, sweet Jesus, Thine—
And bathed in its own blood—
While the firm mark of wrath divine,
His Soul in anguish stood.

Was it for crimes that I had done
He groaned upon the tree?
Amazing pity! grace unknown!
And love beyond degree!

Well might the sun in darkness hide
And shut his glories in,
When Christ, the mighty Maker died,
For man the creature's sin.

Thus might I hide my blushing face
While His dear cross appears,
Dissolve my heart in thankfulness,
And melt my eyes to tears.

But drops of grief can ne'er repay
The debt of love I owe:
Here, Lord, I give my self away
'Tis all that I can do.
—ISAAC WATTS

14

Pray It Forward

The Gift of Perseverance

The essential thing "in heaven and earth" is . . . that there should be long
obedience in the same direction; there thereby results, and has always
resulted in the long run, something which has made life worth living.
—Friedrich Nietzsche, *Beyond Good and Evil*

Do you see what this means—all these pioneers who blazed the way, all these
veterans cheering us on? It means we'd better get on with it. Strip down, start
running—and never quit! No extra spiritual fat, no parasitic sins. Keep your eyes on
Jesus, who both began and finished this race we're in. Study how he did it. Because
he never lost sight of where he was headed—that exhilarating finish in and with God
—he could put up with anything along the way: cross, shame, whatever. And now
he's there, in the place of honor, right alongside God. When you find yourselves
flagging in your faith, go over that story again, item by item, that long litany of hostility
he plowed through. That will shoot adrenaline into your souls! —Hebrews 12:1–3 msg

When Christian was seven years old, he received an ant farm in the
mail. I had never seen anything like it, but Christian had observed
one at school and was very excited. He opened the box very carefully, expecting his ants to be inside. But instead there was an address

to send off to get your ants when you had your ant farm ready.

Okay, a bit of a delay. But nothing we couldn't handle. We sent off for the critters, and every day Christian checked the mail to see if his little buddies had arrived. When they finally did, he was ecstatic.

They were in a test tube with instructions as to how to get them from there into their new high-rise apartment. We very gingerly deposited them into the farm and watched.

Nothing.

"What's wrong with them, Mom?" Christian asked.

"I think they're tired from their journey," I said, looking at the most lethargic group of creepy crawlies I had ever seen in my life. "Just wait until tomorrow; they'll be dancing all over the place."

But tomorrow wasn't much better. Or the next. I decided we had been sent either a bunch of geriatric ants or the most depressed members of the colony. So I put the ant farm on a shelf in the kitchen and we forgot about it for a couple of days until I was cleaning the kitchen.

My, what a change! Not only had the ants perked up, but it seemed as if by magic they had transformed a pile of sand into Las Vegas! It was amazing to see what these tiny creatures had achieved.

We could learn a thing or two from watching them, couldn't we?

GO TO THE ANTS!

Dr. Henry Cloud once told me how God used ants to help him write his doctoral dissertation. He had no desire to tackle this huge research and writing task, so he kept putting it off. But the due date kept getting closer and closer.

One day he heard God tell him in his spirit to go and read a particular verse from Proverbs: "Go to the ant, you sluggard! Consider her ways and be wise" (6:6 NKJV).

Henry said he was a little put out by the word *sluggard* until he realized that one of its meanings is "someone who wants to avoid pain." So Henry bought an ant farm to observe how the ant could help him in his overwhelming task. Initially he, too, was unimpressed . . . until a couple of weeks after they arrived when they had built a whole city—one grain of sand at a time.

Perseverance is a hard discipline to learn. I struggle with it in lots of ways. For instance, in my pantry, I have the basic components of about five diets. I'll stick to one for a few days, and then I'll get fed up and decide it doesn't work and switch to something else. When I am bored with that, I'll throw myself into another, and another.

The sad conclusion I have come to is that every diet program I have works—it's *me* that doesn't work! You see, when I was in my twenties and thirties, I could skip lunch and lose two pounds. Now I have to skip spring!

When it comes to our prayer lives, however, what, if anything, does the ant have to say to us? I think its life and work ethic speak volumes to us. We should aspire to be persistent—as one woman I know was.

PERSISTENCE IN PRAYER

At a Women of Faith conference not long ago, a girl held up a picture and asked me, "Do you remember her?" I looked at the photo of a woman who seemed to be about my age, and I was grateful that I did remember her. She had been coming to the conferences for several years and always asked me to pray for her daughter.

"I do," I said. "Is that your mom?"

"Yes," she replied. "She died a few months ago."

"I am so sorry," I said, saddened that this vibrant woman was gone.

"I was cleaning out her things and I came across your book," her daughter said as big tears began to trickle down her cheeks. "It had her ticket in it for this year, so I came in her place."

We hugged for a few moments. As she left, she called back to me, "See you next year!"

For years her mom was a faithful little ant. Every day she brought her prayer request for her daughter before the Lord and piled prayer upon prayer upon prayer. Now I was the one who got to see the city she was building because she didn't give up. She kept up her long obedience in the same direction and it paid off.

Jesus told a parable to illustrate the importance of never giving up in prayer.

Jesus told them a story showing that it was necessary for them to pray consistently and never quit. He said, "There was once a judge in some city who never gave God a thought and cared nothing for people. A widow in that city kept after him: 'My rights are being violated. Protect me!'

"He never gave her the time of day. But after this went on and on he said to himself, 'I care nothing what God thinks, even less what people think. But because this widow won't quit badgering me, I'd better do something and see that she gets justice—otherwise I'm going to end up beaten black-and-blue by her pounding.'"

Then the Master said, "Do you hear what that judge, corrupt as he is, is saying? So what makes you think God won't step in and work justice for his chosen people, who continue to cry out for help? Won't he stick up for them? I assure you, he will. He will not drag his feet. But how much of that kind of persistent faith will the Son of Man find on the earth when he returns?" (Luke 18:1–8 MSG)

The question Jesus asked those who were listening is very relevant for us: how much of that kind of persistent faith will he find when he returns again? It is easy to get discouraged when we don't receive an answer to our prayers or see any sign at all of change. But Jesus says, "Don't give up. If an old, cranky, godless judge will eventually answer just because he wants to get back to sleep, how much more will God, our loving Father, give you what you ask?"

DON'T GIVE UP

In his book *A Long Obedience in the Same Direction*, Eugene Peterson describes the Christian life as a journey, a pilgrimage that we embark upon one step after another.[1] The principle of "a long obedience in the same direction" is one that is understood in many venues where people experience success.

Weight Watchers has been a successful company for more than forty-five years. It was founded in the 1960s as a discussion group for those who were struggling with their weight. It now operates in more than thirty countries around the world. The basic philosophy is that if you keep taking steps in the right direction, eventually you will reach your goal.

Ironically, the very thing that guarantees them success is the thing that kept me away: slow and steady! I'm always looking for some quick-fix diet, even though if I use my brain I know that slow and steady lifestyle changes actually get me there.

What is it in us that wants a magic wand so we don't have to do the hard work?

Father Martin has worked with those in Alcoholics Anonymous for many years. In one of his videotaped lectures, he tells about a man who came to him and said, "Father, I am a hopeless alcoholic. I've been drinking a quart of vodka, a gallon of Chablis, and a case of beer every day for the last twenty years. I've read a lot of stories in the Bible lately, and I know that Jesus is the master of the impossible. So pray over me and tell Jesus to set me free from bondage."

Father Martin responded, "I've got a better idea. Go to Alcoholics Anonymous, attend ninety meetings in ninety days, find yourself a sponsor, diligently work the twelve steps under his guidance, and read the Big Book every day. In other words, do the hard work."[2]

There are so many examples in Scripture and through Christian history of the effectiveness of faithful dedication even in the most difficult circumstances. Perhaps one of the most well known is Monica, the mother of the great fourth-century writer and theologian Augustine. She was in a very difficult marriage but was determined that her three children would not suffer because of this. She made sure Augustine was able to go to the best schools and have every advantage any other child would be offered. Her greatest prayer was that her children would come to a personal relationship with Christ. In his signature work, *Confessions*, Augustine wrote that his mother "wept to God for me, shedding more tears for my spiritual death than other mothers shed for the bodily death of a son."

Monica had her work cut out for her. Augustine was a very rebellious youth, growing into a man who freely indulged all the lusts of the flesh. His mother despaired of his ever turning around, but when Monica brought her concerns before Ambrose, bishop of Milan, he told her, "It cannot be that the son of those tears be lost."

And so Monica prayed. Finally, when Augustine was thirty-two years old, he gave his life over to Christ. For those thirty-two years, Monica set her face obediently in the same direction and never gave up. And when Augustine finally came to faith, he became widely known as a defender of truth and one of the abiding examples of faith to us today.

Another example of perseverance in prayer is the Shunammite woman from the Bible (2 Kings 4:8–37). She was a wealthy woman who had often extended hospitality to the prophet Elisha, knowing him to be a holy man of God. After some time she said to her husband that she would like to give Elisha his own space in their home where he could have privacy and rest. She was very kind to Elisha and he wanted to do something for her, so he asked her if he could put a favorable word in the king's ear on her behalf. But she thanked him and said no.

Then someone told Elisha her private heartache was that she didn't have a son and her husband was old. Elisha told her that within the year she would have her boy. And she did.

Life seemed perfect until one day, when he was still just a young boy, her son became deathly ill while out in the fields with his father. They immediately rushed him home to his mother. She rocked him in her arms for a few short hours and then the boy died.

This woman took the body of her beloved son and laid him on the bed they kept for Elisha when he was traveling their way. She got a servant and a donkey and set off to find Elisha, who was ministering at Mount Carmel. Somehow this woman believed that through this holy man God had given her the impossible, and so the answer she needed must rest with him as well.

When Elisha heard what had happened, he returned to her home and shut himself in the room alone with the boy. Elisha cried out to God to bring life to this dead son. And God heard his prayers and returned life to the boy.

You might question why I would include a story like this. Yes, I know it's a biblical miracle that few of us would ever experience today. But there is a deeper lesson here too. In D. L. Moody's book *The Joy of Answered Prayer*, he cites this story and encourages those whose loved ones seem to be "dead in trespasses and sins" to never stop praying, because God can breathe new life when it seems as if everything has died.[3]

As you reflect on your own life, where are the places where you have given up hope? It might be praying for a loved one to find Christ. It could be for a child who has wandered away from faith. It might be for yourself. How many of us as women look at an area in our lives that we want to change but it just seems too hard?

PLAY THE MOVIE FORWARD

In Dr. Henry Cloud's book *Nine Things You Simply Must Do*, he describes the principle of playing the movie of our lives forward.[4] Take the example of a woman who wants to lose fifty or a hundred pounds—when you look at that task in cold, hard numbers, it is daunting. But if you play the movie forward six months or a year down the road . . . where is the woman now? Hopefully well on the way to reaching her goal, having worked at it day by day.

What about you? Where would you like to be in six months or a year? And how will you get there? Just as the ant picks up one grain of sand and moves it, then the next one, then the next one—and because of its long obedience in the same direction builds a city—one year from now, we will all be different. We don't get to stay the same, but we do get a choice in how we will have changed, whether it's for the better or not.

In your spiritual lives, too, as you "play the movie forward," where do you want to be in a year's time? If you want to be growing in your faith, closer to God and bold in your prayers, then day by day follow the example of the little ant and set your face in that direction by spending time in God's Word and in worship and prayer every day. Understand it can take time. All good things do. But that's okay, because the journey is worth it.

I know this firsthand. I'm not saying I've completely nailed the perseverance part down myself. I could learn a thing or two from Christian when it comes to that. I love my son's optimism. I tend to have a negative reaction to new challenges, but he has an overwhelmingly positive one. When his soccer coach decided that for the 2007 season Christian should be the team goalkeeper, I dropped to my knees in prayer! He sprang to his feet with confidence. He had never tried to be a goalie before, but that didn't seem to bother him.

His coach told me there was a goalie camp on Wednesday nights and Christian might benefit from it. I asked Christian what he thought and he said, "I think I'll do great without it, Mom, but if it would make you feel better, then I'll go."

I assured him it would make me feel much better. So on Wednesday night, there I was in my ten-dollar folding chair on the sideline cheering him on.

It was clearly more difficult than he had expected it to be—he let in a plethora of goals. When the final whistle blew, he walked up to me and with a straight face said, "This could take some time!"

That's just the way it is. Everything that has value is worth intentional, daily commitment and obedience. I know that it's not easy, but just take the first step, then the next and the next, and before you know it you'll be much further down the road. Make the commitment that in Jesus' name and for his sake, you will embark on a long obedience in the same direction.

God answers prayer, O do not doubt Him;
God answers prayer, believe His Word:
God answers prayer, now venture on Him,
His Word the test of time has stood.

God answers prayer, O soul, believe Him;
God answers prayer, I've proved Him true!
God answers prayer, now venture on Him;
He answered me, He'll answer you.

God answers prayer, fear not to trust Him;
God answers prayer, He longs to save:
God answers prayer, look up believing,
For this His only Son He gave.

God answers prayer, O child so weary;
God answers prayer, pure you shall be:
God answers prayer, His blood availeth;
From self and sin He'll make you free.

God answers prayer, I dare believe it;
God answers prayer, O praise His Name:
God answers prayer, and here this moment,
His love sets all my heart aflame.

God answers prayer in times of trial;
God answers prayer when all seems dark;
God answers prayer, He'll safely guide you,
He loves and "knows the way you take."

—GEORGE BENNARD

15

Overwhelmed with Thanks

The Gift of Gratitude

If the only prayer you said in your whole life was, "thank you," that would suffice. —Meister Eckhart

Make a joyful shout to the Lord, all you lands! Serve the Lord with gladness; come before His presence with singing. Know that the Lord, He is God; it is He who has made us, and not we ourselves; we are His people and the sheep of His pasture. Enter into His gates with thanksgiving, and into His courts with praise. Be thankful to Him, and bless His name, for the Lord is good; His mercy is everlasting, and His truth endures to all generations. —Psalm 100 NKJV

Last night we had a storm here in Frisco, Texas. The sky turned inky black, and the wind picked up the cushions from our garden furniture and donated them to our neighbors. The thunder started as a gentle rumble, like an orchestra tuning up before the maestro takes his place at the podium. The lighting engineer ran a quick test to make sure every area of this vast stage was covered. And then there was a moment of quiet.

I was sitting in bed with the drapes that cover our bay window open, just waiting. Our two bichon frises, Tink and Belle, were fast asleep, one on my pillow and one at my feet. Then, without further introduction or preamble, the show began. The television had been on in the background, but in an instant the screen went black as the satellite signal was knocked out. There was only room for one show in town.

Lightning split the sky in two, and thunder seemed to shake the house. Belle jumped up so quickly she fell off the bed, and Tink stood at the foot of the bed barking at the elements as the wind whipped the trees into a frantic dance and rain battered our windows.

It was spectacular. Two forms of lightning competed like dueling pyrotechnics. Some lit up the whole sky as if God had flipped a master switch in the heavens, and others tore through the sky from heaven to earth like the flash of a sword.

It lasted for about an hour. And then, as quickly as it began, the show was over. I pulled on my boots and put a jacket over my pajamas and went outside to recover our scattered items from various lawns. But before I started, I stood in the middle of my yard and applauded God.

YEA, GOD!

Do you ever have moments like that when you are so filled with awe about God's greatness and power that all you can do is pray, "Yea, God!"? Every Friday night at our conference I watch as the miracle of gratitude and worship transforms exhausted women into delighted daughters. I alluded to this in an earlier chapter, but I am so in awe of these wonderful women who spend their weekends with us that it bears repeating: it takes a lot for a woman to carve out two days for herself. If she has a family, she needs to plan for child care and meals. Jimmy has baseball practice—who will take him? Sarah has a dental appointment and the dog needs to be taken to the groomer. . . . There are so many things a woman does that have to be covered before she can make her way to that seat on a Friday night and flop down with a sigh of relief.

As the worship team takes the stage and invites women to stand with them, I love to position myself at the back of the arena and watch the faces. I usually pick one woman and hone in on her and imagine the internal dialogue that is taking place.

"Won't you stand with us, and let's worship God together!"

"Stand?! Lady, are you kidding? This is the first time I've sat down in a week! I wonder if I should call home and check on things? No, I said I wouldn't do that this time. This is my time; I work hard and I deserve a break. But what if Bob forgot to pick up the dog? They'll charge us a boarding fee, and Sarah will be so upset. Okay, come on, Linda, don't do this, just relax. I wonder if anyone's got any gum. I'm starving . . . I . . . I . . . Ooh, I love this song!"

I watch as "Linda" stands up and in just a few moments is caught up in worship. Everything in her life is still the same as it was. Her family will cope with her absence. Bob will forget to get Jimmy after practice, but he will pick up the dog . . . and order pizza rather than heating up the dinner Linda left. She will have to take the call on Monday morning that will tell her she has to come in for a follow-up visit after her last mammogram. But for now Linda is caught up in what is more real than anything else: she is loving and being loved by her Father and receiving strength for all that lies ahead. As the worship continues and she sees she is part of fifteen thousand women all worshipping together, from the deepest place inside comes a healing prayer of enormous gratitude: *Thank you!* Her face is lifted from the weight of "stuff" she has left at home and is drawn to look at her Father. She forgets for a moment everything that might be wrong with her life and remembers what is always true: she is loved and she is not alone. Worship is gratitude with flesh and bones on it.

Why is gratitude so important? It has become something of a buzz word in our culture. If you Google *gratitude*, you'll be amazed at what pops up. There are whole movements now dedicated to the emotion. I looked at one website that is seeking to sign up a million people worldwide who will commit to taking time every day for intentional gratitude. The site is not linked to personal faith in God; it is just an encouragement to daily choose an attitude of thankfulness. As I read over their documents, I couldn't help but ask, "Who are you thanking?"

Gratitude is not a floating concept. It has to be linked to something or someone before it makes any sense.

One of the first things we taught Christian as a little boy is that when he says thank you to someone, he looks the person in the eye rather than muttering it at his knee caps. And when he writes his thank-you notes (the bane of every mother's life!) after his birthday party, he thanks each person for the specific gift.

When he turned six, we had a big party for Christian with all his first-grade and neighborhood buddies at our home. Before the guests arrived I gave him my gratitude philosophy: "Today you are going to get a lot of gifts. Some of them you will love, some of them you will think are goofy, and some you will already have. If there are duplicates, we'll sort that out later. What matters today is that you thank each person, remembering that the gift comes from the heart whether you like the gift or not."

The very first gift Christian opened, he already had. But he looked at the giver and said, "I love it! Thank you so much!" Then he put it down, came over to me, and whispered in my ear, "How am I doing?" So cute!

BE THANKFUL IN ALL SITUATIONS

I love this encouragement from Paul's letter to the church in Philippi:

> Rejoice in the Lord always. I will say it again: Rejoice! Let your gentleness be evident to all. The Lord is near. Do not be anxious about anything, but in everything, by prayer and petition, with thanksgiving, present your requests to God. And the peace of God, which transcends all understanding, will guard your hearts and your minds in Christ Jesus. (Philippians 4:4–7)

I memorized these verses many years ago, but in my mind I had it categorized as my "Don't worry" verse until Ruth Graham helped me see a much bigger picture than I had previously noticed. I was staying at their home after taping a couple of interviews with Ruth and Dr. Billy Graham. She and I were sitting by the fireside that night talking about favorite books and passages of the Bible, and

Ruth told me this particular text had helped her on many occasions to be thankful in the midst of a storm.

As we chatted, she elaborated on her thoughts and pointed out to me the importance of thanking God as well as bringing our petitions to him. As a mother, she said, when one of her children was going through a difficult time, she would pray with tears for God to intervene—focusing only on the struggle at hand and the need for God's care. But as she studied that text, God illuminated in her heart the importance of thanksgiving even in the midst of the difficulty.

That knowledge, she confided, changed everything for her.

It changed things for me too. It's been liberating! This kind of prayer says to God, "Even though I do not have an answer yet, I trust you. You are good and you are God all the time."

I learned that lesson in a place in which I believed I would learn the least: a psychiatric ward. I've mentioned (and have written about in other books) my struggle with depression and my subsequent time in a hospital.[1] One night while I was a patient there, the nurse's station received a phone call for me from someone I had never met before. The nurse asked if I knew the person who had called. I told her I didn't.

If you call a psychiatric ward and ask for a patient, the hospital will not acknowledge that this person is indeed a patient. What the hospital does do is provide a private line for patients' use, and they can give the number to friends and family if they choose to do so. Later that night the phone rang in the patients' lounge. Someone picked it up and said it was for me. I was surprised because the only person I'd given the number to was my mom and I knew that by now, with the international time change, it was the middle of the night in Scotland. So I immediately feared the worst and assumed something had happened to someone in my family.

I picked up the phone, and a strange voice asked if I was the Sheila Walsh from Christian television. I was thrown by the question, but I must have said yes because of the diatribe that followed. This unknown man told me I was a disgrace to the body of Christ and he would do everything within his power to tell as many people as possible that I was in a mental institution doped up on drugs.

You can imagine how overwhelmed I was by his hatred. I dropped the phone and fell to my knees as sobs racked my body. Everything this man said fed into what I already thought of myself. I felt weak and a disappointment. I was ashamed that I couldn't just pull myself out of the pit I was in. (I later discovered that one of the other patients told their family I was a patient, and the word got around their church until it reached Mr. Happy!) With his words, this stranger had taken every secret thought that rumbled around the basement of my soul and pasted them on a wall in front of me so that I could no longer ignore what I believed to be true.

And though it pained me tremendously at the time, I am deeply thankful for that gift.

Now before you think I might need another wee trip to the ward with locks on the windows, let me explain what I mean— why I believe living with a heart of gratitude no matter what will transform your life. That awful experience came from a thoughtless and judgmental Christian, but my Father God picked it up and used it for good. Everything that man said I had thought, but I hadn't dared voice it out loud. I might have thought I had things well covered, but what is inside us will deal with us until we deal with it whether we like it or not. And as long as those feelings were buried inside me, they continued to emit their peculiar poison. Now that it was all on the table in a way that brought me to my knees, God—with the help of some wonderful Christian doctors and nurses—could begin to heal me of the shame that did not belong to me.

Here is my position as I look at my life today. I believe God is sovereign all the time, not just some of the time. Nothing—absolutely nothing—that comes into your life or my life is a surprise to him. Everything has to pass through his merciful hands. Now, much of the time we don't see it coming, so it knocks us over. But even in that prone place, as we are reeling from what just happened, we can say thank you.

I am not suggesting we just up and move into a place of denial, as if nothing happened. Not at all! What I am saying is that even in some of life's most painful moments deep in my spirit, I thank God. I thank him because he knew it was coming and has provided everything I need to get through it. The saying goes that we're either victims in this world or we are not. If Christ had not come and taken all the sin and hatred on himself, we would be without hope. But he did come and he did die and he did rise from the dead, so we are not victims!

One of my dear friends understands this. Her name is Evelyn Husband—something I love to tease her about: "Did the pastor ask you, 'Do you take Mr. Husband to be your husband?'" But even though she has a wonderful sense of humor and is even kind enough to laugh at my corny question, she has seen some very rough weather too.

You may remember her story: Rick Husband was an astronaut

with NASA in Houston, Texas. He died on February 1, 2003, over the southern United States when the space shuttle *Columbia* and her crew perished during entry, sixteen minutes prior to their scheduled landing. Evelyn was waiting by the landing strip with her daughter, Laura, and son, Matthew. They watched the countdown clock tick backward—and when it got to zero and started counting up again, Evelyn knew something terrible had happened. Yet she says that even in that moment she found herself thanking God for all the Scripture that she and her children had tucked into their hearts and souls. In the days and weeks that followed, some of the astronauts' wives were interviewed on national television, and Evelyn's faith shone like a brilliantly cut diamond through the dark night she was in.

When Evelyn was our guest at Women of Faith the following year, she told us that Psalm 23 had taken on new meaning for her: "Even though I walk through the valley of the shadow of death, I will fear no evil, for you are with me; your rod and your staff, they comfort me" (Psalm 23:4). Eleanor reminded us that for there to be a shadow, there has to be light—that it is not possible to cast a shadow in total darkness. Because of Christ's sacrifice, Evelyn, Laura, and Matthew were able to walk—at times crawl—toward healing. And always with the companionship of the Shepherd. And for that they are eternally grateful.

A GRATITUDE JOURNAL

I don't know what your life is like today, whether you would say you are in the best days or the most difficult days—or perhaps, like me, a mixture of both. I want to suggest that you start keeping a gratitude journal. This is not a prayer journal, which is obviously a great thing to do and something that can greatly enrich your prayer life. Rather, this is just to write down all the things you are grateful for. Our prayer journals reflect our requests, but our gratitude journals can contain how God has answered our prayers or simply be a gateway to wonder and worship. I find it very helpful to use my gratitude journal in prayer. It gives me a written account of the faithfulness and goodness of God. I love to remind God of all the great things he has done!

You might think if you add one more thing to your to-do list, it will push you over the edge and you'll be calling me for the number to the wee place with locks on the windows! Relax, this is not a major undertaking. Just keep any kind of journal by the bed, and each night jot down three things you are grateful for. It can come from a passage of Scripture you read or a friend who called to brighten your day. It can be that when someone said something unkind, you didn't let it take root in your heart but sent it packing. It can be a flower in your yard or the fact that your child realized there is a laundry basket and managed to get her socks into it. You get the picture—it's just a way to refocus away from all the stuff that isn't working and thank God for what is.

But even if you choose not to write in a journal, do take time to be aware of God's mercy and love. Embrace the opportunity to go to him in prayer without any great need or concern but simply to express your gratitude. Each day, in the midst of the madness of everything you need to accomplish, take time to stop and very intentionally turn your face and heart to your Father and say thank you! As I do, let it be your faith declaration that no matter what comes in that day, God is still on the throne and he will hold you and give you all the grace you need.

How good it is to thank the Lord,
And praise to Thee, Most High, accord,
To show Thy love with morning light,
And tell Thy faithfulness each night;
Yea, good it is Thy praise to sing,
And all our sweetest music bring.

O Lord, with joy my heart expands,
Before the wonders of Thy hands;
Great works, Jehovah, Thou hast wrought,
Exceeding deep Thine every thought;
A foolish man knows not their worth,
Nor he whose mind is of the earth.

When as the grass the wicked grow,
When sinners flourish here below,
Then is there endless ruin nigh,
But Thou, O Lord, art throned on high;
Thy foes shall fall before Thy might,
The wicked shall be put to flight.

Thou, Lord, hast high exalted me
With royal strength and dignity;
With Thine anointing I am blest,
Thy grace and favor on me rest;

I thus exult o'er all my foes,
O'er all that would my cause oppose.

The righteous man shall flourish well,
And in the house of God shall dwell;
He shall be like a goodly tree,
And all his life shall fruitful be;
For righteous is the Lord and just,
He is my Rock, in Him I trust.
PSALM 92—THE PSALTER

16

And God Rejoiced

| *The Gift of Trust*

Courage brother, do not stumble, though thy path be dark as night: There is a star to guide the humble, trust in God, and do the right. Let the road be dark and dreary and its end far out of sight. Face it bravely, strong or weary. Trust God, and do. —Norman Schwarzkopf

Trust God from the bottom of your heart; don't try to figure out everything on your own. Listen for God's voice in everything you do, everywhere you go; he's the one who will keep you on track. Don't assume that you know it all. Run to God! Run from evil! Your body will glow with health, your very bones will vibrate with life! Honor God with everything you own; give him the first and the best. Your barns will burst, your wine vats will brim over. —Proverbs 3:5–10 MSG

I could see him through my closed eyelids. (Mothers of young boys can do that.) He must have been six inches away from my face—staring, waiting. I opened one eye.

"Mom, you're awake!" he cried as he leapt into my bed and threw his arms around my neck.

Happy Birthday to you.
Happy Birthday to you.
Happy Birthday, dear Mom.
Happy Birthday to you!

"That was beautiful!" I said.

"It's just you and me, Mom," my son announced with obvious elation. "Dad took Belle to the groomer and then he's going to pick up your cake, which is a surprise."

"Apparently not!" I said.

"Do you want your gift now?" he asked.

"Don't you think it might be more fun to wait until Dad gets back?" I suggested.

"Dad's already seen it," Christian replied. "Plus, I'm not sure I can wait."

For days he had been dropping hints about my gift. The latest tipoff was "poured concrete." I had no idea what he could be making that would require poured concrete.

"It's a brick, isn't it?" The night before my birthday I had guessed while Christian was in the bath up to his eyebrows in bubbles. "You've made me my very own brick!"

"Mom! It is not a brick," he said in a tone that let me know he was rolling his eyes under the foam.

"It's a statue of . . . of . . . . Hamtaro!" I said, wiping a mock tear from my eye at the thought of a statue of our hamster.

"No, Mom, be serious. Maybe when he's dead, but not while he's still boogying on his wheel."

"All right," I said. "I would love to see my present now."

"Come on, Mom. It's in my room!"

I sat up and ran my fingers through my hair. My neck felt "out" and my back was stiff. I thought back on days when I'd awakened and jumped out of bed anticipating the day ahead—and then realized I couldn't actually remember any.

I followed Christian upstairs to his room. Before we reached the door, we were assaulted by a raucous rendition of what sounded like "Give My Regards to Broadway" from Ginger. Ginger is a red-factor canary that we keep in a cage in Christian's room, and she is verbose and perky in the morning. I try not to hold it against her.

She also has an interesting undercover life as a decorator. While the rest of the household is fast asleep, Ginger dons her artist cape and with her black beret fashionably askew on her head, she gets to work. Each morning I climb the stairs abrim with anticipation.

Will it be sweet corn on the walls or apple on the mirror?

Will there be bird food tossed like a Persian rug across the room?

Or will it be lovingly placed like a comforter on Christian's bed?

She never disappoints. One has to admire that in a bird.

In his room, Christian asked me to sit on the floor, close my eyes, and hold out my hands. When he dropped his present into my outstretched arms, I was very glad that I was already sitting on the floor because I would have been going down whether I meant to or not.

I opened my eyes and looked at his gift while he danced around the room like James Brown. It was beautiful. It was a mosaic garden-path stone he had designed himself. In the center, he had written, "I love you, Mom."

"I picked all your favorite colors for the stones, Mom," he said. "I wanted to give you something that you would always have, and I wanted you to know I love you. This way, you can stand on it."

As I write this, it crosses my mind that if I didn't have a son, I would have very little to talk about! There are so many moments in my relationship with Christian when God speaks to me. I don't think that is an accident. The relationship between parent and child is based on trust. The greater the trust the more open and free the child is.

So, too, with our Father—the more we trust him, the greater our freedom.

I received Christian's gift to me as a gift from the heart of a loving boy and a gift from the heart of a loving Father. Every time I look at the stone, I am deeply moved. I am so grateful that at forty years of age I was invited into the adventure of being a mother. More than that, every time I look at this stone, I hear my Father say, "Sheila, you can trust me. I am here and when you can't see my hand, you have my Word—stand on it."

As I have written this book, I have been challenged to take an honest look at how much I trust God.

We live in the visible world. Even though I believe the invisible world, the kingdom of God, is far more real, the visible world is what we see and deal with every day. When we are faced with bills we can't pay or a diagnosis we did not expect, it's hard to remember God is in control and can be trusted all the time. We live in a world where we are barraged with messages about how to take care of our health, our family, and our future. But although it is obviously wise to use common sense and responsibility, our lives ultimately rest in God's hands. Doctors can make well-educated guesses, but God is the one who has numbered the hairs on our head and knows how long our race is. Financial planners can offer good advice, but only God knows what tomorrow brings.

But that is the great news! He is the one who has promised to lead us and to guide us, and he is the one who invites us to come to him in simple trust. As I've heard Max Lucado say, "You have never lived an unloved moment in your life."

THE ABCs OF FAITH

I recently picked up a magazine in my doctor's office and read an article on how to present oneself in conversation to impress the most people. The article recommended extending your vocabulary and general knowledge of world events so that you would appear "well rounded." As I read it I thought, *I am so grateful we get to come to God just as we are.*

Not everyone understands that God welcomes us at whatever stage or age of life we are in. A young woman once wrote to me and asked, "How can I know God hears my prayers? I don't speak very well and I can't read. My prayers might be off." Her question reminded me of a story I read in D. L. Moody's book *The Joy of Answered Prayer.*

The story is about a young boy brought up in an English poorhouse. These Dickensian institutions were for the poorest of the poor in Victorian England. If you have ever seen the movie *Oliver,* based on Charles Dickens's book *Oliver Twist,* then you will remember how grim these poorhouses were.

This boy had never learned to read or write. All he knew were the letters of the alphabet. One day a traveling preacher visited the children and told them that if they were ever in trouble, they should pray and God would answer them and send help.

The boy finally found a job and was apprenticed out to a farmer. His first job on the farm was to take care of some sheep. No matter how hard he tried, he couldn't keep them all together. Remembering the preacher's words, he decided to pray and ask God to help him control the sheep. So he got down on his knees in the field to pray.

Someone passing the field heard a small voice coming from behind a hedge, and when he looked to see who it was, he saw this boy on his knees, reciting the alphabet, "A, B, C, D . . ." He asked the boy what he was doing, and the boy told him he was praying.

The man said, "That's not praying. You're just reciting the alphabet."

The boy told the man that he didn't know how to pray, but he thought if he gave God all he knew, he believed that God could arrange the letters into a prayer for him and give him what he needed.[1]

Wow! Now that is faith. That is trust. And I believe that is prayer!

The point is, God knows you and loves you. He knows what you need before you ever say a word, but it delights his heart when you trust him enough to get down on your knees and pour out your heart. That is a gift of love, and it makes the Father's heart rejoice. Then when you get off your knees and continue through each day living every moment in communion with him, understanding that your whole life can be a gift of open prayer to God, including him in every thought and moment, what a joy to the Father's heart! Your prayers don't have to be clever—far from it. God will take a faltering, simple prayer any day over fancy words with no heart.

The last time I conducted chapel at Christian's school, I told the children that sometimes the simplest prayers are the most powerful. When you find yourself in a rough place or you are too tired to pray, just say the wonderful, lovely name of Jesus.

WHAT DO WE KNOW FOR SURE?

Prayer is the closest we get to life back in Eden. It is the place where we can be most known, the most naked and vulnerable before God.

But you might ask, what does that look like in difficult times? One of the most powerful examples of trust in God's unwavering love is found in the book of Acts. I'm talking about Paul and Silas when they were beaten and thrown into a jail cell in Philippi. They set out for a successful mission's trip and within a day of being in the city were stripped naked, beaten, and thrown into a cell with their feet held down by blocks of wood. We get to look into their jail cell at midnight and catch a glimpse of what was going on.

> About midnight Paul and Silas were praying and singing songs to God as the other prisoners listened. Suddenly, there was a strong earthquake that shook the foundation of the jail. Then all the doors of the jail broke open, and all the prisoners were freed from their chains. (Acts 16:25–26 NCV)

What I find remarkable about this story is that Paul and Silas were at the darkest point of the night in the darkest circumstances they had ever been in, and yet they were singing. Why? Because

Paul and Silas looked at the one thing that had not changed in their situation—God. Everything else around them had gone wrong. They were in pain and their lives were threatened, but they fixed their eyes on what they knew to be true in the invisible world no matter what seemed true in the visible. They stood on the truth that God is good all the time and was watching over them. And even though the angel released Paul and Silas from their chains, they didn't try to escape. They waited and were able to lead the jailer and his entire family to faith in Christ.

We can't always predict the behavior of others, but we can always count on the heart of God.

As I write these words, I know that some of you will be reading them in the best days of your life and some in the worst. Some of you have walked with God for many years and have a track record of his faithfulness in your life. Others of you might be relatively new believers, and trust, though such a small word, can seem like it requires a huge leap of faith. But regardless of the circumstances in your life at the moment, I pray you will know the peace that comes from trusting God loves you and is watching over you.

In his wonderful book *Ruthless Trust*, Brennan Manning writes:

The splendor of a human heart which trusts that it is loved gives God more pleasure than Westminster Cathedral, the Sistine Chapel, Beethoven's *Ninth Symphony*, Van Gogh's "Sunflowers," the sight of ten thousand butterflies in flight or the scent of a million orchids in bloom.[2]

Do you ever think about that? Do you know what it means to our Father and to Jesus our Savior when you choose to trust in

everything? I *love* the truth that we can give back to the One who
has given everything for us by trusting in his love. It is of course a
totally win-win situation, since the One we are being asked to trust
is 100 percent trustworthy, and as we continue to walk with him,
we understand that more and more. It's not that we won't ever be
tested but rather that testing plus trust is love. A time of testing can
paralyze us, but when we mix it with trust, we move out in love.

David knew this. The psalms record many of David's prayers of
trust in God:

> "I will trust in you. In God, whose word I praise, in God
> I trust; I will not be afraid" (Psalm 56:3–4).

> "He put a new song in my mouth, a hymn of praise to
> our God. Many will see and fear and put their trust in
> the LORD. Blessed is the man who makes the LORD his
> trust" (Psalm 40:3–4).

> "I am like an olive tree flourishing in the house of God;
> I trust in God's unfailing love for ever and ever" (Psalm
> 52:8).

I love the image David uses of being a tree flourishing in God's
presence. He doesn't use the image of a flower that will be cut and
wither over time, but a tree that is firmly planted and whose fruit
produces oil. Oil is often used as a metaphor for the Holy Spirit.
As we are planted in God's house, our lives produce fruit and the
Holy Spirit can flow freely from us.

There is no greater gift we can give God than our trust, and
there is nothing more liberating than to do that in prayer. Just as

that little boy brought his ABCs to God trusting that his love would make a prayer out of them, we are invited to bring our lives, our families, our hopes, and our dreams and lay them as a gift before our Father, believing he can be trusted with everything we treasure most. Prayer is the place where we take our hands off our lives—it is trust in action.

When our smaller dog wants to hide her treat from her sister, she finds me and tucks it under my leg. She pushes and pushes with her nose until it is out of sight. It is her way of saying, "This is my greatest treasure, but it's also where I'm most vulnerable so I'm leaving it with you."

Your heavenly Father waits with open arms to hold your treasures. There is no safer place in heaven or on earth.

When we walk with the Lord in the light of His Word,
What a glory He sheds on our way!
While we do His good will, He abides with us still,
And with all who will trust and obey.

Trust and obey, for there's no other way
To be happy in Jesus, but to trust and obey.

Not a shadow can rise, not a cloud in the skies,
But His smile quickly drives it away;
Not a doubt or a fear, not a sigh or a tear,
Can abide while we trust and obey.

Not a burden we bear, not a sorrow we share,
But our toil He doth richly repay;

Not a grief or a loss, not a frown or a cross,
But is blessed if we trust and obey.

But we never can prove the delights of His love
Until all on the altar we lay;
For the favor He shows, for the joy He bestows,
Are for them who will trust and obey.

Then in fellowship sweet we will sit at His feet.
Or we'll walk by His side in the way.
What He says we will do, where He sends we will go;
Never fear, only trust and obey.
—John H. Sammis

17

You Are Not Alone

The Gift of Community

Life is so full of meaning and purpose, so full of beauty beneath its covering, that you will find earth but cloaks your heaven. Courage then to claim it; that is all! But courage you have, and the knowledge that we are pilgrims together, wending through unknown country home. —Father Giovanni Giocondo

Your love must be real. Hate what is evil, and hold on to what is good. Love each other like brothers and sisters. Give each other more honor than you want for yourselves. Do not be lazy but work hard, serving the Lord with all your heart. Be joyful because you have hope. Be patient when trouble comes, and pray at all times. —Romans 12:9–12 NCV

We were never meant to be alone. We are relational beings designed to thrive and blossom in community. Before we had taken our first breath, God looked over the earth he had created and said, "Let us make human beings in our image, make them reflecting our nature" (Genesis 1:26 MSG). The original plan was that just as the Godhead, three in one, live in perfect harmony, so we would walk with God and with one another.

God placed Adam in paradise and then said, "It's not good for the Man to be alone; I'll make him a helper, a companion" (Genesis 2:18 MSG). And so Adam and Eve were connected to God and to each other in perfect union. The invisible world walked hand in hand with the visible. Every breath was a prayer because there was no distance between man and God. There was no sin, no shame, no separateness. Just perfect communion.

Think about that—the ease with which Adam and Eve communed with God. There were no distractions, no bills to pay or dental appointments, no carpool or long lines in the grocery store. There was no sin to pull their thoughts from worship or worry to place a blanket over their souls. There was no miscommunication between them. They walked in peace with God and with each other.

SO LONG AGO IN THE GARDEN

On the day I checked it, Wikipedia defined *prayer* as "An active effort to communicate with a deity or spirit either to offer praise, to make a request, seek guidance, confess sins, or simply to express one's thoughts and emotions."

The word that stands out for me in that definition is *effort*. It can seem like quite an effort to get our thoughts out or even to unravel how we really feel. But it was never supposed to be that way. There was no effort or exertion for Adam or Eve as they talked with God. There was open relationship. Everything was in perfect harmony. Father, Son, and Holy Spirit existed in an unbroken circle, and all Adam and Eve knew was that they were loved.

In the moment they reached out and took fruit from the tree of the knowledge of good and evil, however, humankind unplugged from God. And when God came walking in the garden in the cool of the evening breeze that day, Adam and Eve were not to be seen.

God asked, "Where are you?"

It's easy upon first read to take that phrase at face value, but I don't think for a moment God didn't know Adam and Eve were hiding behind a tree. I think God's question was for them to take a look at themselves and see where they now were.

Adam answered, "I heard you in the garden and I was afraid because I was naked. And I hid" (3:10 MSG).

Ah, such sad words. For the first time in human history, someone tried to hide what he was ashamed of from God. Perfect communion—unbroken, effortless prayer—was gone.

God asked Adam, "Who told you you were naked?" Again, God knew the answer—but he wanted Adam to see what broken communion looks and feels like.

And as if all he'd already done wasn't horrible enough, Adam blamed Eve and God. He told God it was Eve's fault and then reminded God that he gave Eve to him.

In a moment, we had lost what was in the heart of God for us: the perfect union that exists between Father, Son, and Holy Spirit. Now we were separated from God by our sin and thrown out of the garden. Cherubim and a revolving flaming sword were set at the gate so we would be unable to reenter. I used to see that as a punishment, but now I realize that removing Adam and Eve from the garden was probably the first act of grace extended to sinners. God knew if Adam or Eve found their way back into the garden and ate from the tree of life, then they would live forever in their fallen state (Genesis 3:22–23). The heart of God would never let that happen because now we were broken.

But God did not want us to live forever in our brokenness. He put a time limit on the detour we would have to take on our way back home. Across many miles, through deserts and hunger, to a land of milk and honey, to prophets and kings, through freedom and captivity, he led us up through the Via Dolorosa to a place called Golgotha, where with staggering love and mercy, for the first time the Godhead was divided as Jesus took into his perfect sinless body the sins of the sons of Adam and daughters of Eve. Until, having absorbed every last vestige of our sin, he cried out, "It is finished!"

And the veil in the temple was ripped from heaven to earth so that men and women could again come into the presence of God in the cool of the evening breeze and walk and talk with him.

Not everything has been restored. The path leads down from that place of sacrifice, and those who walk on it, though covered by the blood of the Lamb, still bear the marks of Adam. They walk through divorce and death, through cancer and betrayal, through the death of dreams and the disappointments of life. But it is not forever. There will be a day for every child of God when the detour we are on will lead us home.

Until then, one of the greatest gifts on our journey is the gift of each other. We were not designed to make this trip alone. Unfortunately, we're not prone to be vulnerable to each other or to take advantage of each other's help.

PRAYING WITH UNVEILED FACES

Adam and Eve's first instinct when they broke communion with God was to cover themselves, and we have been doing it ever since. Even as believers, although we say we are saved by the blood of Christ alone, we hide who we really are from God and from each other. Shame still lies deep at our core, and just as Adam tried to blame Eve and Eve blamed the serpent, we have been convinced from that moment onward that love is conditional and that we fall far short of the conditions.

I overheard a conversation one day between two people who were discussing the book of Genesis and comparing that world to our culture today. The gentleman said, "Adam and Eve were ashamed of their bodies and tried to cover them. Now we don't care who sees our bodies. We just cover our faces so no one can see into our souls."

I think that is profoundly true. We try to conceal the parts of our lives we are not sure make the cut—something that can be especially true in our prayer lives. I used to be afraid to pray in public in case I said the wrong thing. What if my theology was wrong or I stumbled over my words? Whenever I had to pray in public I would rehearse my words over and over in my head to see if everything sounded right and made sense. Then I'd worry it sounded like I had been practicing, so I'd make myself stumble over a part of it.

Yes, I agree, it was ridiculous. When I think about it now, I have to smile. Prayer was never supposed to be an audition but rather open and honest communication between a Father whose love knows no end and his children. And it was designed to allow us vulnerability before our fellow believers. But I chose not to allow others to see me.

All the "professional" prayers ended, however, when I found myself soaked to the skin in the companionship of brokenness.

During my hospital stay, I began to enjoy what it feels like to come as a child and talk with other children to our Father. No one in a psychiatric ward is trying to impress anyone else—the jig is pretty well up at that stage! So our prayer time was a moment of honesty not just before God but before each other. This was new to me. To allow others into your brokenness is something humbling and yet liberating. To me, it's characterized by two things: praying *for* one another, and praying *with* one another. Each is vitally important to our sense of community, so let's take a look at them.

Standing in the Gap—Praying for One Another

Each morning after breakfast in the psychiatric ward, my new friends and I would meet in the patients' lounge, join hands in a circle, and pray for one another. For the first few days I couldn't pray, but I was deeply moved by those who prayed for me.

- "Dear Father, help Sheila today to find the courage to face the truth about her life knowing that you love her."

- "Dear Father, help her to face her fear and not to be afraid to cry."

- "Dear Father, thank you for bringing her to a safe place. Help her to feel safe today."

I cannot tell you what those simple, profound prayers meant to me. After all the years I had lived as a believer, for the first time I began to experience what it feels like to be part of the body of Christ. And soon I was able to offer my own prayers for my companions—simple, perhaps halting, but heartfelt. And I

213

could see that my prayers for them were gratefully received too.

Looking back, I can't believe I spent so long trying to impress people with my prayers, as if I were applying for a job! Prayer is not supposed to put walls between us; it is supposed to break them down. Over and over in the New Testament, we are encouraged to pray for each other.

⋅❯ "Make this your common practice: Confess your sins to each other and pray for each other so that you can live together whole and healed. The prayer of a person living right with God is something powerful to be reckoned with" (James 5:16–17 MSG).

⋅❯ "Every time you cross my mind, I break out in exclamations of thanks to God. Each exclamation is a trigger to prayer. I find myself praying for you with a glad heart" (Philippians 1:3–4 MSG).

⋅❯ "And pray for us, too, that God may open a door for our message, so that we may proclaim the mystery of Christ, for which I am in chains" (Colossians 4:3).

Only when I was broken enough to put aside my rehearsed prayers was I truly able to experience what a joy it is to pray for others—to think of something and someone else. And to feel how prayers impacted not only others but me.

Standing Side by Side—Praying with One Another

God has always called us to walk out our faith as a people—not as individuals but as a group. When he called the Israelites out of

Egypt, he called them to come out together, not one by one. The Psalms were written as corporate liturgy to be sung together as a community. Jesus told us that he is returning for a bride, who is all of us in the body of Christ.

This means that not only is prayer our personal means of communication with God, but it is a way for us believers to come together as one. Never, ever underestimate the power of praying together. The Bible tells us:

→ "Take this most seriously: A yes on earth is yes in heaven; a no on earth is no in heaven. What you say to one another is eternal. I mean this. When two of you get together on anything at all on earth and make a prayer of it, my Father in heaven goes into action. And when two or three of you are together because of me, you can be sure that I'll be there" (Matthew 18:18–20 MSG).

→ "Through the Spirit they urged Paul not to go on to Jerusalem. But when our time was up, we left and continued on our way. All the disciples and their wives and children accompanied us out of the city, and there on the beach we knelt to pray" (Acts 21:4–5).

→ "Everything in the world is about to be wrapped up, so take nothing for granted. Stay wide-awake in prayer. Most of all, love each other as if your life depended on it. Love makes up for practically anything" (1 Peter 4:7–8 MSG).

I hope you've had the opportunity to truly pray in a communal experience. If not, I encourage you to give yourself that gift. There is nothing like it. As I experienced with my fellow patients, it is fellowship at its barest and most powerful. And it is life changing. For me, the closest relationships I have are the friends I pray with. Prayer is acknowledging the invisible in the presence of the visible, and I believe the evil one trembles when he sees God's people on their knees together.

Perhaps, like me, you are afraid to pray in public or to offer prayer for a friend because you have no confidence in your prayer skills. Let me ask you a question: if a child you loved with all your heart came to you and with faltering words said, "I love you such a bunch!" Would you despise that sentiment because it wasn't articulated properly?

Of course not! Your heart would be moved, and you would reach down and embrace that child.

That is how our Father sees us.

Now, it is possible that someone in a prayer group some time might look down on your style of prayer or lack of polish. But who cares what other people think! Prayer is not about impressing other people. It's about loving God all the way home . . . just like my friend Eric.

A BEAUTIFUL LIFE

Eric Kuntz was born September 7, 1983, to Steve and Karen Kuntz. The doctors were concerned about his health and did a chromosome test. Three weeks later, the results came back positive for Down syndrome. In an e-mail to me, his mother, Karen, wrote:

I remember my first thought after I hung up the phone. It was "God, show me what to do!" He was our firstborn. We did not know how to raise a "normal" baby, let alone a baby with challenges. Every expectant parent just assumes they will have "the perfect Gerber baby." NOTHING can prepare you for the death of your dreams of a perfect child. Although we cried, our tears were more for our baby than for us. We never asked, "Why us?" We were actually thankful that WE were given him by God instead of parents who would not be able to care for him. We knew Eric would have to struggle to learn even the simplest tasks. He would be made fun of, stared at, never get married or have children.

I met Karen and Eric at a Women of Faith conference in Des Moines, Iowa. Since then I've been able to spend time with Eric now and again, and each time he touches my life deeply. In my office I have several drawings he drew for me, and they remind me of his precious spirit.

Des Moines is a consistent stop in the Women of Faith conference schedule, and one year Karen and I arranged a time for the three of us to get together before the weekend began. Eric and Karen met me at my hotel on the Thursday night. I wish I could show you a picture of this young man's smile. There is a gentle grace about him and a deep abiding sense of the presence of God and his angels.

I asked Karen to write down some thoughts on her son's life. Here's what she said:

Eric's faith in God is so apparent and real. He puts on no pretenses. He does not cover up what he feels. People have told me they can tell he loves the Lord, his face just shines! Eric loves to go to church and Sunday school. He fully participates in the worship service and "sings" along with the hymns. He has absolutely NO sense of pitch, but either he cannot tell, or just does not care. HA! He is always two or three seconds behind everyone else, but pours his heart into it. People can tell when we are in church—HA!

He is a real "people reader." He can sense when someone is sad or not feeling well. When he looks at me when I am sad it is like he can see into my soul and feel it too. He cries when someone else cries (even if he doesn't know why he is crying).

Eric is grateful for little things. Sometimes he will pop up with "Thank you for food" after making him dinner or "Thank you for ride," when we go somewhere. At large extended family gatherings he will make everyone stop eating, put down their silverware, and prays, "Thank you for food. Amen!" After he was really sick last December, he came up behind me, hugged me, and said, "Thank you taking care of me when I sick."

Eric was diagnosed in 2006 with severe sleep apnea. The Greek word *apnea* literally means "without breath." People with untreated sleep apnea stop breathing repeatedly during their sleep, sometimes hundreds of times during the night and often for a minute or longer. Many people are able to be treated for this illness, but Eric has not responded to any management option. The family has tried every treatment available and is having no success. The doctor told Karen it was amazing Eric was still with them. He said, "God has a special purpose for Eric that has not yet been fulfilled." And so for Karen and her husband, every breath that Eric takes comes with a prayer of thanksgiving from the family.

I asked Eric that night what it is like when he gets really sick. He said, "When I sick, angels close to me. They love me; hold me, kind to me." (Eric appears to have had an ongoing experience with the other side of the veil. Karen told me that when he was a baby he was very sick, but his memory of that time is, "Jesus held me and rocked me.")

On the Saturday of the Des Moines conference, I requested two VIP seats for Eric and Karen, as I wanted them in the front row where we could see each other. At breaks I would go over to Eric, and we would hug each other and talk about what he had enjoyed so far. He said, "With you and with everyone, we sing!"

When it was my turn to sing and speak, I dedicated my last song, "Find Your Wings," to Eric: it talks about a mother's love for her son and her prayer that God would fill his heart with dreams.

Eric never took his eyes off me. He smiled widely, even with tears running down his face. But what I found even more moving was our final time of corporate worship. Twelve thousand members of the body of Christ stood together and raised their voices to God our Father. I looked across the stage at my friends, and at that moment it was clear that we were no longer Eric who had Down syndrome, Linda who was waiting for test results, and twelve thousand other women, each with their own struggles and celebrations, disappointments, and dreams—we were family, one voice singing our praises together.

There is a mystery at work here, and if we are not careful, we will miss it. If we will grasp hold of the truth that this road we are walking on is a broken place, a detour on the way to where our real lives begin, we might begin to see one another differently. God has wrapped some of his most amazing people in unusual packages, and I urge you not to miss one of them. Some of us are fat or thin; some tall or short; some physically, mentally, or emotionally handicapped; but we are all challenged in one way or another. And we are a family, a community. As long as we are on this path, it is our joy and strength to hold on to one another, pray for each other, and sing our hearts out whether we are in tune or not!

The Church's one foundation
Is Jesus Christ her Lord,
She is His new creation
By water and the Word.
From heaven He came and sought her
To be His holy bride;
With His own blood He bought her
And for her life He died.

'Mid toil and tribulation,
And tumult of her war,
She waits the consummation
Of peace forevermore;
Till, with the vision glorious,
Her longing eyes are blest,
And the great Church victorious
Shall be the Church at rest.

Yet she on earth hath union
With God the Three in One,
And mystic sweet communion
With those whose rest is won,

With all her sons and daughters
Who, by the Master's hand
Led through the deathly waters,
Repose in Eden land.

O happy ones and holy!
Lord, give us grace that we
Like them, the meek and lowly,
On high may dwell with Thee:
There, past the border mountains,
Where in sweet vales the Bride
With Thee by living fountains
Forever shall abide!
—SAMUEL J. STONE

Prayer Is Who We Are

It was my hope as I began this book that through the process of research and study, my own prayer life would be stretched and strengthened. What I didn't anticipate was that every area of my life would be touched. It has become so clear to me that I can't separate my prayer life from my life as a wife and mom, a friend, a writer, a speaker, or a woman.

Prayer is not just something we *do*—it is who we are. On our knees or as we walk through each day, prayer is our birthright. Our ongoing conversation and relationship with God through the sacrifice of his Son, Jesus, defines us. All the Father has ever wanted is unbroken relationship and love between his heart and ours. Because of Christ's sacrifice, there is no one keeping a list of what we get right and what we get wrong. We are invited every moment of every day to live in his presence.

When my son saw the title of this book, he asked me, "Is it wrong to pray on your knees, Mom? I thought that was one of the best ways!" My answer to him is my heart for you: there is no greater gift that we are given on this earth, after our salvation, than the open line we have directly to the heart of God. There are moments when all we want to do is kneel. There are moments when all we can do is lay on our faces and call on the name of Jesus. There are moments when we want to stand with our faces toward the warmth of the sun and talk with our Father or battle against the driving rain as we share our hearts with him. The point of the title is that rather than something we do and then mentally tick off our list like picking up the dry cleaning, prayer is our life, our very breath. Share everything you love and everything that troubles you with him. Sing, cry, scream, laugh, dance, and rejoice always, knowing you are in his presence, loved and received.

This doesn't mean every prayer will be answered as we might hope it would, but there is a day coming when this detour will end and we will be home free. Until that day we have our Father who loves us, our Savior who died for us, and the Holy Spirit who intercedes for us when we don't know what to say. And we have each other. Christ is not returning for a foot or a hand but for a glorious bride. We are the body of Christ, rich or poor, young or old, eloquent or stumbling. And when we give our lives to him, we can experience a life where we get off our knees, lift our hands in the air, and pray until we see him face to face.

notes

Chapter 1: What Does the Bible Actually Say about Prayer?
1. This quote, along with other information about Dana Carvey and his character the Church Lady, is available at http://en.wikipedia.org/ wiki/Dana_Carvey, accessed 2 June 2007.

Chapter 2: Why Is Prayer So Important?
1. See, for example, *The Heartache No One Sees: Real Healing for a Woman's Wounded Heart* (Nashville: Thomas Nelson, 2007) and *Life Is Tough, But God Is Faithful: How to See God's Love in Difficult Times* (Nashville: Thomas Nelson, 2001).

Chapter 3: Why Is It So Hard to Pray?
1. Guy H. King, *Prayer Secrets* (London: Marshall Morgan and Scott, 1955).
2. C. S. Lewis, *The Screwtape Letters* (San Francisco: HarperSanFrancisco, new ed. 2001), 39.

Chapter 5: Why Does God Say No?
1. Nancy Guthrie, *Holding on to Hope: A Pathway Through Suffering to the Heart of God* (Carol Stream, IL: Tyndale, 2006).

Chapter 6: Is God Angry with Me?
1. William Blake, "To the Deists," *Jerusalem,* The Illuminated Books of William Blake, vol. 1 (Princeton University Press, rep. 1997), 213.

Chapter 7: Why Does God Seem Absent when I Pray?
1. Sheila Walsh, *Honestly* (Grand Rapids: Zondervan, 1997).

Chapter 12: Are You Asking Me to Let Go?
1. Sandi Patty, *Falling Forward . . . into His Arms of Grace* (Nashville: Thomas Nelson, 2007),
2. John Kavanaugh, *America* 173, 29 July 1995.

Chapter 13: Lay Your Burdens Down
1. Richard Foster, *Prayer: Finding the Heart's True Home* (San Francisco: HarperSanFrancisco, 1992), 37.

Chapter 14: Pray It Forward

1. Eugene Peterson, *A Long Obedience in the Same Direction: Discipleship in an Instant Society*, 20th Anniversary ed. (Downers Grove, IL: InterVarsity, 2000).
2. Father Martin's *Chalk Talk*, circulated in AA for over thirty years; available at http://www.sobrietyfirst.org/audio.htm.
3. D. L. Moody, *The Joy of Answered Prayer* (New Kensington, PA: Whitaker House, 2002), 10.
4. Henry Cloud, *Nine Things You Simply Must Do: To Succeed in Love and Life* (Nashville: Integrity Publishers, 2004), chapter 5, "Play the Movie."

Chapter 15: Overwhelmed with Thanks

1. For more about Sheila's struggle with depression, see her book *Honestly* (Grand Rapids: Zondervan, 1997), available at www.sheilawalsh.com.

Chapter 16: And God Rejoiced

1. D. L. Moody, *The Joy of Answered Prayer* (New Kensington, PA: Whitaker House, 2002), 105.
2. Brennan Manning, *Ruthless Trust: The Ragamuffin's Path to God* (San Francisco: HarperSanFrancisco, reprint ed. 2002), 2.

WOMEN OF FAITH®

Women of Faith, North America's largest women's conference, is an experience like no other. Thousands of women — all ages, sizes, and backgrounds — come together in arenas for a weekend of love and laughter, stories and encouragement, drama, music, and more. The message is simple. The result is life-changing.

What this conference did for me was to show me how to celebrate being a woman, mother, daughter, grandmother, sister or friend.
— Anne, Corona, CA

I appreciate how genuine each speaker was and that they were open and honest about stories in their life even the difficult ones.
— Amy, Fort Worth, TX

GO, you MUST go. The Women of Faith team is wonderful, uplifting, funny, blessed. Don t miss out on a chance to have your life changed by this incredible experience.
— Susan, Hartford, CT